W9-CMD-803

# The Skills of Teaching:

## Interpersonal Skills

**Robert R. Carkhuff, Ph.D.**

**David H. Berenson, Ph.D.**

**Richard M. Pierce, Ph.D.**

CARKHUFF
INSTITUTE
of HUMAN
TECHNOLOGY

**Andrew H. Griffin, Ed.D.**

National Education Association

**Carolyn M. Schoenecker, M.A.**

American International College

# Teacher's Guide

*Human Resource Development Press*

Publishers of Human Technology

CARNEGIE LIBRARY
LIVINGSTONE COLLEGE
SALISBURY, N. C. 28144

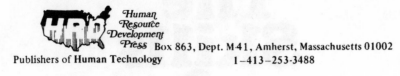

*Human Resource Development Press* Box 863, Dept. M41, Amherst, Massachusetts 01002

Publishers of **Human Technology**     1–413–253-3488

Copyright © 1977 by Human Resource Development Press, Inc.

All rights reserved. Printed in the United
States of America. No part of the material
protected by this copyright notice may be
reproduced or utilized in any form or by
any means, electronic or mechanical,
including photocopying, recording, or by
any information storage and retrieval
system, without written permission
from the copyright owner.

International Standard Book Number: 0-914234-51-X
Library of Congress Number: 74-75374
First Printing – Sept. 1977

*Designed and Illustrated by Tom Capolongo*
*Consulting Editor, David V. Rowland*
*Consulting Art Director, Eileen Donovan*

1.0

371.102    C 277, 2

118792

## UNIT 6:  INITIATING SKILLS

## UNIT 7:  PREPARING YOUR LEARNERS FOR LEARNING

## UNIT 8:  EXAMINATIONS AND GRADING

This Teacher's Guide has been developed to help college professors and in-service teacher educators use The Skills Of Teaching: Interpersonal Skills. It is based upon our 15 years of experience teaching these inter-personal skills to thousands of teachers.

Unit I will help you plan your course, familiarize you with what the Guide contains and explain how it is organized. Units 2 through 7 detail suggested teaching techniques and exercises, plus a summary of key con-cepts for each chapter. Unit 8 offers several ways of evaluating your students' learning - including both skill and knowledge assessments.

We sincerely hope we have saved you time in your class and workshop preparation and perhaps added an idea or two to your teaching outlines.

August, 1977
Amherst, Mass.

R.R.C.
D.H.B.
R.M.P.
A.H.G.
C.M.S.

## ABOUT THE AUTHORS

DR. ROBERT R. CARKHUFF is Chairman, Carkhuff Institute of Human Technology (CIHT). The author of more than two dozen books on helping and teaching effectiveness, Dr. Carkhuff is internationally renowned as the most-cited reference in the last decade in counseling psychology. Dr. Carkhuff is the developer of the human and educational resources development models upon which The Skills of Teaching series is based.

DR. DAVID H. BERENSON is Director of Educational Technology, CIHT. Teaching for more than 15 years at primary and secondary grade levels, Dr. Berenson has spent the last 10 years revolutionizing pre-service and in-service teacher training programs. He has conducted pathfinding research in the development of effective educational delivery systems. Dr. Berenson is co-author of the entire Skills of Teaching series.

DR. RICHARD M. PIERCE is Director of Human Technology, CIHT. His specialty is conducting in-service teacher and counselor training programs. Dr. Pierce is noted for his extensive research on the training of teachers and counselors. He is the co-author of Helping Begins at Home and Teacher as Person.

DR. ANDREW H. GRIFFIN is Instructional and Professional Development Specialist, liaison with NCATE and AACTE, National Educational Association. Dr. Griffin is spearheading a national effort to improve the level of teaching skills of primary and secondary level teachers in addition to helping teachers eliminate the effects of racism and sexism in the classroom.

MS. CAROLYN M. SCHOENECKER is a Graduate and Undergraduate Instructor for the Department of Human Relations, American International College.

# UNIT 1: Teacher's Guide Introduction And Overview

We've all heard statements along the lines of "So-and-so is just a natural teacher!" Such statements, pointing to some innate and mysterious capability, really reflect nothing so much as the speaker's own lack of experience. For people are not born with an ability to teach effectively - they create that ability in themselves through concerted effort and constructive training. And the cornerstone of all such effort and training may be summed up in a single word: skills.

There is always some element of the mysterious or the unexpected in human interactions, of course. People are not simply machines. Yet even as the medical profession has learned to heal the human body, exchanging the often irrational mumbo-jumbo of earlier ages for the clinical diagnoses and modes of treatment of modern medicine, so teachers have begun to recognize the specific and observable activities which can effectively promote human learning. In so doing, they have not sought to reduce their students to less-than-human automatons. Rather, they have sought to promote their own effectiveness by developing a greater repertoire of substantive skills and responses. The Skills Of Teaching: Interpersonal Skills represents the authors' efforts to support just such a process of development.

The Skills Of Teaching: Interpersonal Skills is designed for use by all students who are or will be involved in teaching delivery in their own working, living or learning settings. Students who are preparing for careers in teaching - whether at pre-school, elementary, high school, vocation or college levels - will find the text particulary useful. The skills taught will help teachers in urban and rural setttings, working with students who are rich, poor, black, white, male or female. This Teacher's Guide is designed for your use in working with any of the above students.

You will find that the Guide provides you with a detailed, step-by-step set of procedures for teaching the substantive materials in The Skills Of Teaching: Interpersonal Skills itself.

This introduction is divided into two major sections:

BUILDING THE COURSE OUTLINE
USING THIS TEACHER'S GUIDE

The first of these sections, "BUILDING THE COURSE OUTLINE," offers some suggestions as to the way in which your course can be constructed. You will find this material useful in clarifying your course goals and achieving these same goals. Several sample outlines are provided to give you an idea of what can be done in interpersonal skills training courses aimed at different goals.

The second section, "USING THIS TEACHER'S GUIDE," suggests specific ways in which you can deal effectively with the basic ingredients of your course: exercises, lectures, assignments, applications, modes of evaluation and so on. A review of this section will help you determine how you can best achieve the particular goals you have set for your course. In addition, such a review will enable you to decide how and where in the course you will introduce specific ingredients.

## BUILDING THE COURSE OUTLINE

There are, to begin, several different levels of goals around which you might structure your course. Your determination of an appropriate goal-level will be affected by such considerations as expected teacher/ student ratio and the length of time allotted for your course. We will present three different goal-levels along with some comments on their relationship to the above considerations.

A survey goal. Here students are presented with a "picture" of the interpersonal skill levels and are given some opportunity to try out appropriate behaviors. Such a goal could be readily achieved within the context of a typical one-credit course lasting 15-20 hours. In addition, most typical teacher/student ratios would lend themselves to achievement of a survey goal. Yet as you will quickly recognize, there are definite limitations to a goal set at this rudimentary level. Students working toward a survey goal cannot be expected to achieve minimal levels of skill acquisition since "trying out" a given skill does not directly translate to sustained skill behaviors.

An acquisition goal. Here students are trained in the basic skills to the point where they have developed a minimal level of skill functioning appropriate for brief interpersonal contacts. In general, such a goal would be appropriate for a course involving 35-45 hours of work with one teacher (or one graduate assistant) for each 15-20 students.

An application goal. Here students progress beyond the simpler survey and acquisition levels and learn to apply the skills in a meaningful ongoing fashion within a career specialty area such as education or counseling. The optimal schedule here would involve a two-course sequence of 80-90 hours in length. This would give students ample time to develop, practice and apply their new skills in ongoing contacts and to combine these new skills with others already developed in their career specialty areas. The best teacher/student ratio for a course structured around an application goal would be to have one teacher (or one graduate assistant) for every 15-20 students.

The following are sample outlines showing how general areas of concern might be treated within courses structured around one or another of the three goals.

## COURSE 1: SKILLS SURVEY (15-20 HRS.)

| Activity | Time |
|---|---|
| Introduction and Assessment | 1 hour |
| Attending Skills | 3 hours |
| Responding Skills | 4 hours |
| Personalizing Skills | 4 hours |
| Initiating Skills | 3 hours |
| Lecture | 2 hours |
| Evaluation, Feedback and Review | 1 hour |
| Total: | 18 hours |

## COURSE 2: SKILLS ACQUISITION (35-45 HRS.)

| Activity | Time |
|---|---|
| Introduction and Assessment | 1 hour |
| Attending Skills | 7 hours |
| Responding Skills | 10 hours |
| Personalizing Skills | 10 hours |
| Initiating Skills | 6 hours |
| Lecture | 3 hours |
| Evaluation, Feedback and Review | 3 hours |
| Total: | 40 hours |

## COURSE 3: SKILLS APPLICATION (80-90 HRS.)

| Activity | Time |
|---|---|
| Introduction and Assessment | 1 hour |
| Attending Skills Training | 8 hours |
| Attending Skills Application | 4 hours |
| Responding Skills Training | 10 hours |
| Responding Skills Application | 5 hours |
| Personalizing Skills Training | 10 hours |
| Personalizing Skills Application | 5 hours |
| Initiating Skills Training | 10 hours |
| Initiating Skills Application | 5 hours |
| Supervision | 6 hours |
| Lecture | 8 hours |
| Problem-Solving Module | 2 hours |
| Program-Development Module | 4 hours |
| Evaluation, Feedback and Review | 3 hours |
| Total: | 81 hours |

You may find it helpful to take a closer preliminary look at the various ingredients presented in these three sample course outlines.

Introduction. There are two things you can accomplish during the brief introductory segment of your course. First, you can give students a helpful overview of the course: where they're going and how they're going to get there. And second, you can conduct a pre-test assessment which will provide both you and your students with a behavioral reference point from which to start the interpersonal skills training.

Skills training. This will obviously be the key concern of your course, regardless of the goal-level you have selected. In planning this training, remember that the four basic skill-areas are cumulative and inter-dependent; thus any attempt to minimize or omit training in one area will inevitably reduce the meaning and value to the students of their training in other areas. In general, you may find that the best arrangement involves spending approximately 20% of the training time on attending skills, 30% on responding skills, 30% on personalizing skills and 20% on initiating skills.

Application training. Students working at this goal-level will need ample time to rehearse, implement, review and revise their application techniques. A typical arrangement might involve devoting about 20% of the time to applications.

Lecturing. While most effective interpersonal skills training programs emphasize "hands on" learning procedures, there is no denying the value of teacher lectures. By focusing on the research and models from which the skills were derived and the ways in which the skills have been applied, such lectures can promote students' understanding of the skills and their real importance. To give your lectures a research-based perspective, you might wish to refer to Kids Don't Learn From People They Don't Like (Aspy, D. N. and Roebuck, F. N., Human Resource Development Press, Amherst, Massachusetts, 1977) which outlines the extensive research base for the Carkhuff Model in teaching.

Evaluation, Feedback and Review. You and your students will need to devote time to assessing, understanding and consolidating all that students have learned at any given point. Unless students have a chance to view their progress in objective terms, they may lose track of where they really are and where they need to go.

Now let's move on to the second section of this introductory unit and consider some of the ways in which you can put this Teacher's Guide to use.

## USING THIS TEACHER'S GUIDE

Units 2 through 7 of the Teacher's Guide are designed to provide you with ideas and methods for running your actual course. Unit 2 focuses on the introduction of course materials and the initial evaluation of students' level of functioning. Units 3 through 6 deal in turn with the substantive skills of attending, responding, personalizing and initiating in relation to the classroom. Unit 7 provides a summary of the materials and focuses upon the concluding evaluation of students' performance.

Units 2 through 7 are developed around didactic, experimental and modeling modes of teaching. Each Unit contains an introductory section, sub-sections for each sub-skill or activity and a summary of the unit with which that chapter is concerned. Within each Unit you will find specific suggestions on the following:

1. Teaching chronology
2. Skill(s) introduction
3. Pre-testing exercises
4. Major teaching points to make
5. Skill(s) demonstrations
6. Practice exercises for large and small groups
7. Possible applications
8. Post-testing exercises
9. Homework assignments
10. Additional instructional points

In addition, you will find suggestions concerning discussions and audio/video-tape demonstrations which may be quite helpful. (You should also note that, in Units 2 through 7, the term "students" is used to refer to your own students while the term "learners" refers to the children, teenagers or adults whom your students will instruct in their own classrooms.)

We'll take a moment to consider each of the ingredients listed above.

Teaching chronology. The presentation of each sub-skill within a given chapter of the Teacher's Guide is prefaced by a brief "teaching chronology." This chronology presents, in numerical order, the major ingredients you will want to include in your treatment of the sub-skill. The numbers given in the chronology correspond with the numbers accompanying specific suggestions outlined on subsequent pages. Thus in the chronology provided for the first sub-skill in Unit 2 ("Attending Physically"), item #1 reminds you to have the students take pre-test; and #1 on the page which follows outlines one way in which you might give a simple pre-test to your class.

Skill(s) introduction. Early in each unit and sub-unit, you will find suggestions for introducing the skill

to students and hooking it up with their own experience of the world. These introductory discussions or exercises will help your students to achieve a fuller preliminary understanding of the skill in question.

Pre-testing exercises. Every sub-unit includes a suggestion as to a simple pre-test procedure that you can use. These exercises will help both you and your class by assessing students' ability prior to each new phase of training. Knowing where they really are often awakens students to the necessity of developing and applying new and higher order skills.

Major teaching points. Throughout each unit and sub-unit, you will find each skill briefly summarized and explained: what it is, what it does, why it's important for teachers, how it's put to use in the classroom and how it fits with other skills. You should add to these points any additional information from the relevant sections of The Skills Of Teaching: Interpersonal Skills which you feel is important.

Skill(s) demonstrations. Once you have introduced a skill and pre-tested students, you will want to show them what that skill looks or sounds like in actual use. You will find references in the Guide to appropriate pages in The Skills Of Teaching: Interpersonal Skills as well as suggestions about things you might do or bring with you to demonstrate the skill. Specific audio and videotape suggestions are also provided here.

Practice exercises. Each sub-unit within a unit contains suggestions on individual, dyad, small-group and large-group tasks with which these are concerned. In general, large-group exercises alone will satisfy the needs of most classes structured around a survey goal. Courses focusing on application or acquisition goals should involve students in as many levels of practice as possible - certainly small - group as well as large-group exercises.

Applications. Since students will find their new interpersonal skills valuable outside as well as inside the classroom, you will want to consider a variety of possible applications with them. In the Guide you will find numerous suggestions for identifying, discussing and practicing specific applications.

Post-testing exercises. If pre-testing motivates students by showing them their limitations, post-testing invariably gives them a shot of confidence by showing them exactly what they have acquired through training. The exercises provided in the Guide will give both you and your students a chance to assess and evaluate growth within specific skill-areas.

Homework assignments. Reading and practicing assignments are provided for students at the end of each unit of work outlined in the Guide. Both types of assignments will reinforce your students' learning and increase the likelihood that they will understand and be able to use specific skills within their own classrooms.

Additional instructional points. Scattered throughout Units 2 through 7 you will find specific instructional points set off in boxes. These points should help you answer student questions and facilitate student acquisition of particular skills. To the extent possible, these points are located at the place in the lesson where you may find them most useful.

Unit 8 contains multiple-choice and short-answer questions related to each chapter in the text. You can use these questions to assess your students' understanding of the didactic materials presented in The Skills Of Teaching: Interpersonal Skills. In addition, Unit 8 offers several ideas on pre- and post-program materials, in-class performance and tests for use in assigning grades to your students.

So much for introductory materials. As a college teacher planning to offer a course on interpersonal teaching skills, you should now have a good idea as to the way in which such a course can be structured and handled. Needless to say, no attempt was made in this Introduction to focus on specific skills or training procedures. The Skills Of Teaching: Interpersonal Skills deals with the skills in ample detail; and the remainder of this Guide outlines a number of effective procedures. In the end, these two components - plus a personal mastery of and ability to use interpersonal skills and a commitment to delivering the same skills to students - are all you really need.

You know that truly fine teachers aren't born that way. Such teachers are people who deliver to students the real skills that they themselves have already developed. We all know that no one can give what she or he doesn't have. In your case, however, you already possess the interpersonal skills that can really make a difference in the classroom. Now, with The Skills Of Teaching: Interpersonal Skills and this Teacher's Guide, you have the systematic materials you need to transform each of your students into a skilled teacher in her or his own turn.

# UNIT 2:  TEXT INTRODUCTION AND DEVELOPING THE LEARNING MODEL

# SUMMARY OF KEY CONCEPTS FOR CHAPTERS 1 AND 2

Concept:     Interpersonal Skills –
The act of relating to the
learner's experience of
learning.

Principle:     If the teacher relates to
the learners' frame of
reference, then the learners
will be able to relate better to their own learning
experience so that the
learners will be able to
learn more effectively.

Skills Goals:     Learning the skills that
make up interpersonal skills.

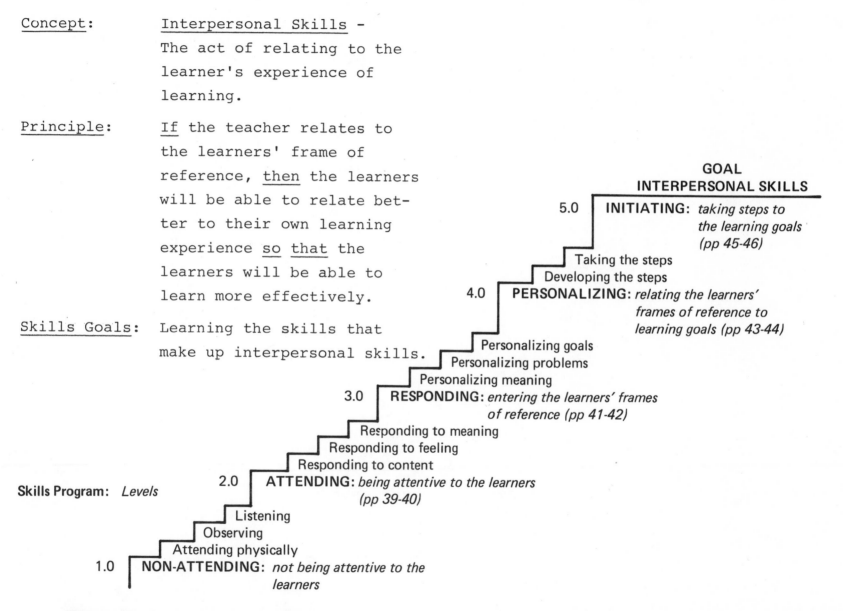

GOAL
**INTERPERSONAL SKILLS**

5.0     **INITIATING:** *taking steps to*
*the learning goals*
*(pp 45-46)*

Taking the steps
Developing the steps

4.0     **PERSONALIZING:** *relating the learners'*
*frames of reference to*
*learning goals (pp 43-44)*

Personalizing goals
Personalizing problems
Personalizing meaning

3.0     **RESPONDING:** *entering the learners' frames*
*of reference (pp 41-42)*

Responding to meaning
Responding to feeling
Responding to content

2.0     **ATTENDING:** *being attentive to the learners*
*(pp 39-40)*

Listening
Observing
Attending physically

1.0     **NON-ATTENDING:** *not being attentive to the*
*learners*

**Skills Program:** *Levels*

**Skills Feedback:** *Pre-Test     (pp 17-32)*

## CHAPTERS 1 AND 2: TEXT INTRODUCTION
## AND DEVELOPING YOUR LEARNER RELATIONSHIP
### (Pages 1 - 47)

## OUTLINE OF SUGGESTED TEACHING CHRONOLOGY

1. Provide brief overview of course.

2. Help students relate interpersonal skills to previous experiences.

3. Get students to identify interpersonal skills.

4. Have students take pre-test.

5. Provide feedback to students.

6. Develop the learning model.

7. Summarize critical components of interpersonal teaching skills.

8. Assign homework.

# INTRODUCTION TO THE CARKHUFF INTER- PERSONAL TEACHING SKILLS MODEL

1. Briefly orient your students to the course content. You may point out that teachers must have many skills, among them the interpersonal skills to develop effective learning relationships with their learners.

2. Discuss with students their past experiences of teachers' inter- personal skills in the classroom. How have these experiences af- fected what they learned? Which teachers did they learn the most from?

## SAMPLE REACTION

"Everybody loved science in 7th and 9th grades. And it was because Mr. Wells worked so hard with everybody. He discussed the subject with you like he liked you. And he paid attention to you when you spoke to him."

## SAMPLE REACTION

"High school math teachers were such a bore. They were always more interested in sports than math. I never got anywhere when I asked them for help. If it hadn't been for my friend Joanne I'd have flunked!"

3a. Ask your students to list the behaviors they think make up good interpersonal skills. You might write their suggestions on the board.

b. Summarize their ideas by pointing out that interpersonal skills involve verbal and non-verbal communication between people.

4. Read your students the learner statements on pages 17 and 18. Ask students to write their most helpful response to the learners. Have students rate the responses on pages 20 and 21 using the scale provided on page 19.

5a. Tell students that effective interpersonal activity involves <u>responsiveness</u> to communicate understanding and <u>initiative</u> to provide guidance.

b. Ask students to check out their discrimination ability by using the explanation and exercise on pages 23 and 24.

6a. Help your students to develop the learning model the class will be studying by asking them a series of questions.

1) "What is the first thing a learner must do when she begins a new task?" (Accept any answers which indicate the learner must search to learn as much as possible about herself and the task. Then explain that this is called <u>exploring</u>.)

2) "Why do we want to help our learners learn about them-selves as well as the task?" (Accept any which indicate the learners must gain a perspective on what they want to be able to do or accomplish in the task. Then explain that this is called <u>understanding</u>.)

3) "Why is it important to help our learners to identify what they are trying to accomplish?" (Accept any answers which indicate the learners must act to achieve their goals if real learning is to occur. Then explain that this is called <u>action</u>.)

b. Organize the learning skills by drawing Figure 2-1 on the board.

**PHASES OF LEARNING**

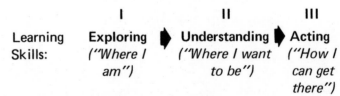

Figure 2-1. **The Phases of Learning**

c. Identify the teacher's interpersonal skills by asking students;

1) "What might a teacher do to help learners feel comfortable exploring themselves and the task?" (Accept any answers involving non-judgmental attitudes of acceptance, understanding and/or warmth. Then explain that this is called <u>responding</u>.)

2) "What might a teacher do to help a learner gain a better understanding of herself in relation to a task?" (Accept any answers involving the teacher's use of her own experience of the learner to provide insights. Then explain that this is called <u>personalizing</u>.)

3) "What might a teacher do to help learners act?" (Accept any answers related to facilitating action. Then explain that this is called <u>initiating</u>.)

d. Organize the teacher's skills by modifying the chart on the board to create Figure 2-2.

**PHASES OF LEARNING**

| Teacher: Helping Skills | Attending | Responding | Personalizing | Initiating |
|---|---|---|---|---|
| Learner: Learning Skills | | Exploring | Understanding | Acting |

Figure 2-2. **How the teacher's helping skills facilitate student learning**

7. Make sure your students know the following things about interpersonal skills:

a. All teaching is done in the context of an interpersonal relationship.

b. Interpersonal skills are the communication skills that allow you to develop the learning relationship.

c. Interpersonal skills make a difference in terms of what and how your learners learn in your classroom.

8. Have students read pages 1-47, <u>Skills of Teaching: Interpersonal Skills</u>. Point out that pages 26-31 will give them a fuller explanation of the levels of responses to learners.

# UNIT 3: ATTENDING SKILLS

## SUMMARY OF KEY CONCEPTS FOR CHAPTER 3

Concept: <u>Attending</u> - the act of being attentive to the learn-
er.

Principle: <u>If</u> the teacher attends to
the learners, <u>then</u> the
teacher will give her full
and undivided attention <u>so</u>
<u>that</u> the teacher can take
in all of the cues concerning the learners' experience.

Skills
Objective: Learning the skills that
make up attending.

**Skills Program:** *Steps*

**OBJECTIVE
ATTENDING SKILLS**

**LISTENING:** *hearing the learners*
*(pp 75-78)*

Reflecting content

Repeating verbatim

Listening for content

**OBSERVING:** *seeing the learners*
*(pp 65-74)*

Drawing inferences for appearance and behavior

Viewing behavior

Viewing appearance

**ATTENDING PHYSICALLY** *(pp 55-64)*

Making eye contact

Leaning

Squaring

# CHAPTER 3:  ATTENDING SKILLS
(Pages 48-85)

## PRELIMINARY POINTS

Attending really means giving learners the kind of attention they have been asking for since schools were invented.  Your students need to know that attending means giving attention; that you give attention by physically presenting yourself so that you can observe and listen; and that giving attention gets attention.

## STIMULUS SUGGESTIONS

To help your students relate to the skill of attending from their own frame of reference, ask how many of them as learners ever:

"Asked a question and got an answer that didn't help, asked it again and got another answer you could not use, then quietly withdrew and said to yourself 'Aw, forget it! You don't understand!  You didn't hear a word I said!'"

"Chatted away with a neighbor in the back of the room until the teacher appeared at your side, big as life, then looked up, meekly picked up your pencil and got back to work."

"Were your bravest self in front of the rest of the class when the teacher was busy getting things out of the supply closet or when she was called out of the room for a minute or two?"

Have your students describe experiences they have had relating to a teacher's attending skills.

For example:

"You knew when to whisper if the teacher was not looking or not in a position to see you."

"You were especially careful to sneak a look at a paper on the next desk only when the teacher was writing on the board or bent over some other student across the room."

Show your students the following
figure:  (You may want to have
mimeograph copies made of Figure
3-1 to hand out to your students.)

**ATTENDING**

The skills involved in attending to learners

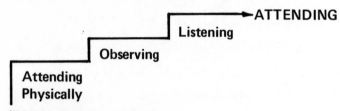

"*Much of what you know
about your learners is a function
of what you have observed in
their behavior and heard in their
expressions.*"

Figure 3-1. **Pre-Teaching Skills**

# CHAPTER 3:  ATTENDING PHYSICALLY
## (Pages 55-64)

## OUTLINE OF SUGGESTED TEACHING CHRONOLOGY

1.   Have students take pre-test.
2.   Have students relate skill of attending physically to previous experience.
3.   Demonstrate and describe steps of how to perform the skill.
4.   Role-play attending physically in the classroom.
5.   Undertake small-group practice and model-building.
6.   Apply the skill of attending physically to the students' lives.
7.   Summarize the critical components of attending physically.
8.   Assign homework.
9.   Discuss pre-test.
10.  Conduct post-test.

1-2. Demonstrate several typical class-room positions a teacher may take during the course of a period. Ask the students to judge their effectiveness (use a rating scale - page 51). Be sure to include demonstrations involving sitting, standing and working with a whole class and with individuals.

3a. Develop a list of effective ingredients of attending postures. Be sure to include these:

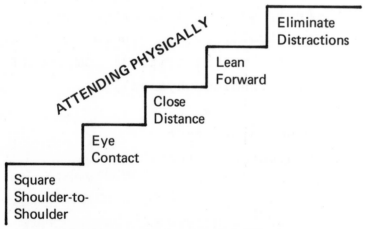

Figure 3-2. **Steps to take in attending physically**

You may want to put these steps on the chalkboard or overhead projector.

b. Examine pictures on pages 48, 58 and 59. How do these rate using the list of steps?

> Students may wonder how you maintain good attending with an extremely active learner. Do not chase the learner around. Rather, position yourself to be able to remain within 3 to 4 feet of the learner as she moves about.

4a. Have several students come up and role-play attending physically in different school situations. The class can critique one another by talking the demonstrator into a "more effective" physical attending position.

b. Your students can check themselves out by:

1) Using the steps one at a time.

2) Asking themselves: "Can I see and hear everything my learners say and do?"

c. Ask students to attend physically to you using all of the steps. Give them feedback on their performance.

Students often feel initially uncomfortable when attending physically - especially in individual interactions with learners. If your students are "hung up" about attending physically, respond to some of their feelings and the reasons for their discomfort. They may feel attending physically is "not real" for them or that it is aggressive and may scare the learners. You can discuss the fact that many learners associate physical attending with negative attention because it is so often their only experience of receiving close attention from the teacher. Remind students that they may be uncomfortable simply because it is a new behavior for them. Attending physically is for the learners:

if used effectively, it will decrease classroom problems.

5. Break the class into small groups of 4 to 6 people. Ask them to prepare several demonstrations of effective physical attending during different teaching tasks. Include situations such as:

> Small Group Reading
> Cafeteria Duty
> Art Activity Period
> Learner Working at a Machine

Attending physically during each task should be spelled out as a list of steps to take. This is so that everyone can do it just as well as the presenter. Ask groups to make presentations to the whole class. Class can use rating scale on page 84 to give feedback.

6. Ask students to generate a list of times and places, other than school, where they could use the skill of attending physically. Discuss the implications in terms of how attending physically might affect personal situations.

7a. Tell your students that attending sets the stage for teaching. It is a pre-condition of effectiveness.

"IF YOU ATTEND WELL PHYSICALLY, THEN YOU WILL BE IN A POSITION TO OBSERVE AND LISTEN WELL ENOUGH TO RESPOND EFFECTIVELY."

b. Before you go on to the post-test, you may want to have the students summarize the skill of attending physically. You can do this by having them fill in the following summary form using pages 55 -64 in their text.

c. After students have filled out their individual summaries, you may want to synthesize their efforts into a master summary on the chalkboard or overhead.

8. Possible Homework Assignments.

a. Ask students to watch 10-15 minutes of a television series and count the number of times the actors attend physically to one another when talking and the number of times they do not attend physically when talking to each other.

b. Have students attend physically to another person for about 30 seconds during a conversation, then quit attending for the next 30 seconds, then return to attending physically and finally record the reaction of the other person to attending and non-attending behavior.

c. Students should study for one-half hour using the steps of attending physically to focus on their learning material. Then they should study one-half hour without attending (e.g., lying down with a T.V. on). Which was a more effective study posture? How would that translate to learners in a classroom?

d. Students should read pages 55-64 Skills of Teaching: Interpersonal Skills.

9, Spend a few moments reviewing the
10, pre-test; then administer the
11. post-test on pages 80-82 and provide feedback related to the progress students have made.

# ATTENDING PHYSICALLY - SUMMARY

| | |
|---|---|
| What is it? | (Giving individual attention to your learners.*) |
| What does it do? | (Communicates openness and readiness.) |
| Why do it? | (Lets learners know you are interested in them.) |
| How is it done? | (1. Square shoulder-to-shoulder. |
| | 2. Make eye contact. |
| | 3. Close distance. |
| | 4. Lean toward your learners. |
| | 5. Eliminate distractions.) |
| When/Where do you do it? | (Whenever you want to communicate interest.) |
| How do you know if you've done it right? | (If you see and hear everything the learners say and do and you get attention back, you've done it right.) |

*NOTE: possible answers in parentheses

# CHAPTER 3:  OBSERVING
### (Pages 65-74)

## OUTLINE OF SUGGESTED TEACHING CHRONOLOGY

1. Relate skill of observing to the students' previous experiences.
2. Review the skill of attending physically.
3. Have students take pre-test.
4. Demonstrate and describe the steps of how to perform the skill.
5. Role-play the skill of observing.
6. Do small-group observing practices in classrooms.
7. Identify uses of the skill of observing outside of the classroom.
8. Summarize observing.
9. Assign homework.
10. Discuss pre-test.
11. Conduct post-test.
12. Provide feedback to students.

1.  Show your class a slide of a classroom of learners.  Ask them to look at the picture carefully.  Shut off the slide and discuss what students saw.  What did they learn about the learners from the slide?  Focus your discussion on the amount students learned by simply using their eyes.

2.  Explore with students the things they did to learn from the picture.  Did students physically attend to the picture?  What did they look for?  What kinds of conclusions did they draw?

    Make sure your students know that observing will combine with attending physically and listening to give and get the attention needed for learning in the classroom.

    You may want to draw Figure 3-3 on the board.

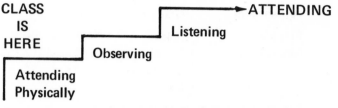

Figure 3-3. **Attending: Getting Ready to Teach**

3a.  As a way of gathering input, ask the students to look at the picture on page 34 and write down what they know about this learner.

b.  Have students share what they wrote.  List their observations in 3 columns on the board (appearance, behavior and inferences - but don't label them yet!)  Get as many observations as possible for each unlabeled column.  Now label the columns and relate the label for each to the type of observations it contains. (See Figure 3-4)

| **Appearance** | **Behavior** | **Inferences** |
|---|---|---|
| Female Blond Hair | Looking through a magnifying glass. | Feels curious-intrigued |

Figure 3-4. **Example of observations**

c. Ask the students to look at what they wrote and decide whether they had all three types of observations. You may want to get a show of hands for the number of students who had 1-2-3 of the types of observations.

4a. Your students need to know the following things about observing: it involves accurately seeing the non-verbal cues learners send out; it will be the richest source of cues for responding to learners as individuals.

b. Develop a list of the components of effective observing. Be sure to include the components in Figure 3-5 (you may want to put them on the board).

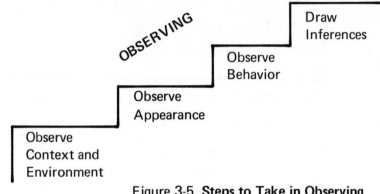

Figure 3-5. **Steps to Take in Observing**

c. With students, develop lists of things to observe at each step. Students can place this information in their notes (see Figure 3-6).

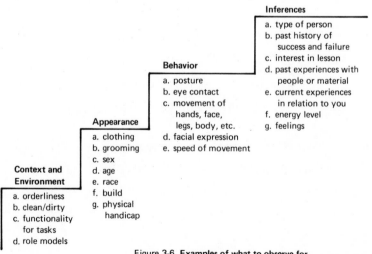

Figure 3-6. **Examples of what to observe for**

> Students need to know that observations are the things we perceive with our senses. Inferences are the conclusions we draw. Thus you _observe_ that Susan is jumping up and down, laughing and talking rapidly. You _infer_ that she has a high energy level.

| OBSERVATIONS OF: | | INFERENCES ABOUT: | | |
|---|---|---|---|---|
| | | Energy Level | Relationship to me as Teacher | Relationship to Material |
| Context and Environment | | | | |
| Appearance | | | | |
| Behavior | | | | |

Figure 3-7. **A helpful format for recording observations and inferences**

d. Use the exercise on page 71. Read the examples of self-observation on the page. Have students make observations about themselves and share them. Students should use the format on page 72.

5a. Tell your students to look at the picture on page 70. Ask them to pick out one of the learners and write an observation using Figure 3-7. You may wish to put the figure on the board. Be sure to have students include at least one observation in each category.

> It is important for students to understand that they want to observe context, behavior and appearance _before_ making inferences. The inferences will only be accurate and useful if they are based on a large amount of observational information.

As individual students share their observations and inferences, the rest of the class should add additional observations and provide feedback on the accuracy of one another's observations.

b.  Pair students. Have them silently make and record observations on one another as they role-play teacher/learner interactions. Use the model in Figure 3-7 for recording observations. Students can share and critique each other's observations. Encourage students to focus on the accuracy of teacher observations leading to inferences about learners' energy level, relationship to the teacher, relationship to the learning activity and feelings, as these greatly impact classroom learning.

Observations, when shared, can be harmful as well as helpful. As the teacher, you must determine the effects of your students sharing their observations. Your students may worry about sharing observations with learners and harming the learners. Observations, like all inter-personal skills, are meant to be used constructively. If observations cannot be em-ployed helpfully, they should not be shared.

c.  Discuss the skill of observing a group of learners as well as observing individuals. Look at the picture on page 74 and use the model in Figure 3-7. Have students record observations and inferences on the class of learn-ers shown. Share and critique observations.

Audio-Visual Options

Option 1: Show several slides (4-6) of different classes during dif-ferent activities. Have students make observations of each slide.

Option 2: Show several slides of the same class during different activities. Have students make observations of each slide.

Option 3: Show several slides of the same class doing one activity at different time periods. Have students make observations.

Option 4: Run four 3-minute segments of a videotaped classroom inter-action. Have students make observations of 2 learners and a group.

6a. Divide students into several small groups (4-6 members). Each group should choose a class activity or subject and develop a list of the most important observations and inferences on learners during that activity.

Examples of activities: recess, lunch, assembly, different sub-jects: music, spelling, science.

Example of important observations and inferences: Gym class, going ice skating - Do all learners have gloves, warm socks, shirts, coats? Amount of movement? Facial ex-pressions? Learner interest in skating? Level of skating skill? Comfortable skates? Energy level? Feeling?

b. Each group should role-play the activity while various students practice observing the learners. Then students should write their observations and share them with the entire group.

7. Have the class develop a list of other times and places where observing can be useful, particu-larly in home and non-teaching work situations. What are some of the possible implications of using observing in these other situations? What are some of the possible things students could observe for?

Example:

Watching a child come home from school - can you tell what kind of day the child has had?

Greeting your date or spouse - what is his/her energy level or relationship to you?

8a. Tell your students that observing is one of the attending skills that prepare you to teach your learners effectively.

"IF YOU EFFECTIVELY OBSERVE YOUR LEARNERS' NON-VERBAL CUES, THEN YOU WILL LEARN WHERE THEY REALLY ARE SO THAT YOU CAN IDENTIFY WHO IS HAVING DIFFICULTY."

b.  Have students summarize the skill of observing using the summary form on the next page and pages 65 to 74. You might synthesize their efforts into one master summary on the chalkboard or an overhead.

c.  Have each student make an observation of the class and write it down.  Get a few students to share their observations.

9.  Possible Homework Assignments:

a.  Visit a classroom.  Make 3 observations of individual learners and record the observations.  Also make an observation of the class as a group.

b.  Read pages 65-74

10,  Briefly review the results of
11.  input from step 3. Then have the students look again at the picture on pages 34 and write what they know about the learner.  Compare the results of the two exercises.

12.  Point out that students have increased their ability to make accurate and comprehensive observations.  They now have a skill rather than random intuition. Reinforce the idea that, as teachers, they will be looking for learning behavior - i.e., attending behaviors - from their learners. Just as attending is getting ready to teach, attending is also getting ready to learn.

# OBSERVING - SUMMARY

**What is it?**
(Seeing your learners as individuals in the learning context.)

**What does it do and why do it?**
(Helps you pick up their non-verbal cues.)

1. Identify learners who are having difficulty.
2. Identify learner's feelings.
3. Prepare self to respond to learner's feelings.

**How do you do it?**

1. Observe context and environment.
2. Observe appearance.
3. Observe behavior.
4. Draw inferences.

**When/Where do it?**
(During all classroom sessions.)

**How do you know if you've done it right?**
("Can I recall observations and inferences for individual learners?")

# CHAPTER 3: LISTENING
## (Pages 75-78)

## OUTLINE OF SUGGESTED TEACHING CHRONOLOGY

1. Have students relate skill of listening to previous experiences.
2. Have students review previous skills.
3. Have students take pre-test.
4. Demonstrate and describe steps of how to perform the skill.
5. Role-play listening in the classroom.
6. Hold small-group practices of listening to learners.
7. Apply the skill of listening to the students' lives.
8. Summarize the critical components of listening.
9. Assign homework.
10. Discuss pre-test.
11. Conduct post-test.
12. Provide feedback to reinforce growth.

# LISTENING

1a. Play two 3-minute videotape segments of a classroom interaction during which the teacher and learners interact. In the first segment, show a teacher whose classroom statements do not reflect any real ability to listen to her students. In the second segment, show a teacher whose statements indicate that she listened to what her learners said.

b. Discuss the differences between the two classroom interactions with your students. What was the difference between the teachers? What would be the learners' experience with each type of teacher? Which teacher would have a more coopera- tive classroom? Which learners would be likely to be more interes- ted in the class?

2. Ask students to identify which teacher used better attending and observing skills. How did that relate to the teacher's listening?

3a. To learn how accurately your students normally listen, read them a short learner statement. Ask them to write exactly what they heard. (Short learner statements can be found in Unit 8 - Skill Assessments.)

b. Have several students read what they heard. Then re-read the original statement. Ask students to identify if they heard it just as the learner said it or if they made changes in their heads as they listened.

To learn how accurately your students are capable of listening when they concentrate, tell them you are going to read another short learner statement. Ask them to attend to you physically, to observe you as you read and then to write down what they heard.

Have several students read what they heard. Then re-read the original statement. Ask students to identify if they heard it just as the learner said it or if they made changes in their heads as they listened.

(You may want to get a show of hands on who heard the statement accurately and who did not.)

4a. With your students, discuss the importance of the teacher <u>listening</u> in a learning situation. If possible, write the reasons on the board.

Possible Reasons for Listening:

1) "Guides you in determining the learner's readiness to get involved in the lesson"

2) "Helps identify learner interest"

3) "Learn important things about your learner in relation to task-needed materials, resources, feelings"

4) "With attending and observing, it prepares the teacher to respond to the learner's experience in learning"

5) "Communicates the teacher's interest in and concern for the learners and their learning"

6) "Your reaction to your learners is important to them only if they know you understand where they are coming from"

b. With your students, develop a list of the effective ingredients of listening. Be sure to include these:

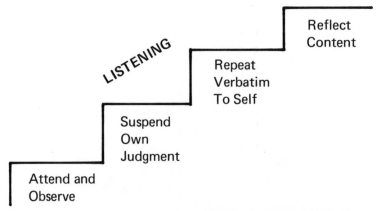

Figure 3-8. **Steps to take in listening**

c.  Ask your students to look at page 75 and read the second paragraph. Discuss other examples of suspending judgment when teaching.

> It is important to suspend judgment initially. A listener is not a judge. Suspending judgment helps the teacher to avoid distorting or misunderstanding what the learner says.

5a. Read aloud the learner statement on page 76 while students attend physically to you. Ask them to write verbatim what they heard. Have 2-3 students read what they wrote while other students identify which students got it verbatim and which did not.

> Practicing verbatim recall will increase your students' ability to listen and suspend judgment. It will also prepare them for reflecting the content.

b.  Have students work in triads. Each student takes a turn role-playing teacher and learner and doing steps 1, 2 and 3 of the exercise given on page 76.

c.  Develop the idea of listening for the gist of longer learner statements. Make sure students understand that learner feelings and questions about needed materials or assistance are important to hear.

Audio-visual Option

Play 20-40 seconds of an audio tape which contains a longer learner statement. Ask students to write the gist of what the learner says. Have a few students share what they heard. Ask the other students to identify anything important that was left out.

d.  Pair students in dyads. Do steps 4, 5 and 6 of the exercise on page 76. Tell students they can check themselves out by asking

"Can I recall the words the learner used?" If they can't recall the exact words, they probably didn't hear them!

e. Study formats given on page 77 for other ways a teacher can check out the accuracy of listening skills in the classroom. See if students can identify any other useful formats.

f. Demonstrate listening in the classroom. Have 2-3 students role-play learners and make statements. Use the formats suggested on page 77 and check out your listening with students after they speak. Make sure you attend and observe as you do so.

g. Ask 1-2 students to demonstrate listening while the class role-plays learners.

6a. Break class into small groups (4-6). Students should practice effective listening in different learning situations (e.g., reading class, field trip, math). As teachers, students should reflect back to their learners the statements their learners make (see page 77).

b. Ask 1-2 groups to demonstrate classroom listening to the class. Students can give feedback about anything important which is left out.

7. Ask the class to generate a list of other times and places where listening could be useful to them. Discuss the importance of listening in these situations. Example: as a learner in the class; talking to a friend; listening to instructions at work.

8a. Summarize listening with your class. Have them write a summary using the form on the next page.

"LISTENING IS HEARING THE IMPORTANT THINGS YOUR LEARNERS SAY. IF YOU LISTEN WELL TO YOUR LEARNERS, YOU WILL BE PREPARED TO RESPOND TO THEM AND THEIR LEARNING."

# LISTENING - SUMMARY

|  |  |
|---|---|
| What is it? | (Hearing what the learners have said.) |
| What does it do? | (Prepares you to respond to learner's learning experience.) |
| Why do it? | (1. Helps you determine learner's readiness to learn. <br> 2. Communicates interest and concern in your learners.) |
| How do you do it? | (1. Attend and observe. <br> 2. Suspend your own judgment. <br> 3. Recall verbatim. <br> 4. Reflect on content of learner's expression.) |
| When/Where do it? | (Whenever learners speak and before beginning any task.) |
| How do you know if you've done it right? | (If you can recall the words your learners used.) |

b. Ask students to share their summaries as a way of checking out their under- standing.

9.  <u>Possible</u> <u>Homework</u> <u>Assignments</u>:

a.  Ask your students to watch a T.V. show such as "Welcome Back Kotter" or "Room 222" and rate the teacher's listening based on how often he or she reflects back understanding.

b.  Have students practice listening in their other classes.  Ask them to write 2-3 statements they could have made as learners which would have reflected what they heard back to the other learners.

c.  Read pages 75-78.

10,
11. Recall with students how many were able to listen accurately when the lesson started (steps 4 and 5). Repeat steps 4 and 5 to learn how many can now listen well.

12. Discuss the ways this growth can be useful to students and increase their competence as teachers.

# CHAPTER 3: SUMMARY OF ATTENDING

1. Recall major points of attending. Include these points:

a. Attending physically, observing and listening are the skills of attending in the classroom.

b. Attending allows you to learn what you need to know about your learners in order to teach them.

Audio-visual Option

Show 5-10 minutes of a classroom interaction. Ask your students to do 3 things:

1) Rate the teacher on her physical attending behaviors and support their rating.

2) Observe the class for context and environment, appearance and behavior and make inferences on feeling, relationship to teacher and relationship to material.

3) Rate the teacher on listening ability and support their rating.

Share and discuss assignment after all students have finished.

2. Break class into small groups (4-6). Ask each group to prepare a demonstration that illustrates "ideal" levels of attending in a classroom. Include physical attending, observing and listening by both the "teacher" and "learners." Have each group demonstrate for the whole class.

3. Have students develop a list of 3 additional places where they can use attending and how they will attend. Use the model below for the assignment.

|  | Where | How to Attend |
|---|---|---|
| Home Situation |  |  |
| Work Situation |  |  |
| Community Situation |  |  |

4. Summarize attending by reviewing the steps on the next page. (You may

want to put these on the chalkboard
or an overhead projector.)

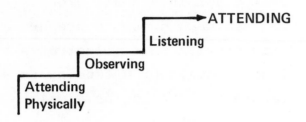

"If you attend effectively, you
will be ready to teach your
learners."

Figure 3—9. **Pre-Teaching Skills**

5.   Possible Homework Assignments:

a.   Review pages 48-85.

b.   Have students practice physical
attending, observing and listening
in their own classrooms.  They
should write a rating and reasons
for the rating of their own
attending at the end of each day.
If possible, you can visit students'
classrooms and provide feedback
on their attending.

c.   If students do not have classroom
teaching responsibilities, have
them practice attending in their
work or home settings and rate
their performance.

# UNIT 4:  Responding Skills

Concept:    Responding - the act of entering the learners' frames of reference.

Principle:    If the teacher responds to the learners' frames of reference, then the learners will know where they are in relation to the learning experience so that the teacher will be able to relate the learners' frames of reference to the learning goals.

Skills
Objectives:    Learning the skills that make up responding skills.

**OBJECTIVE**
**RESPONDING SKILLS**

**RESPONDING TO MEANING:** *giving the reason for the feeling (pp 114-119)*

Reflecting feeling and meaning
Complementing feeling with meaning
Asking the reason questions

**RESPONDING TO FEELING:** *attaching the feeling to the learners' experience (pp 95-113)*

Reflecting feelings
Formulating feeling words
Asking the feeling questions

**Skills Program:** *Steps*

# CHAPTER 4: RESPONDING SKILLS

(Pages 86-124)

## PRELIMINARY POINTS

Remind the class that attending behaviors are the interpersonal skills which get you ready to teach. Attending gets and gives the attention students need and want if they are to learn.

Responding is letting your learners know verbally that you understand them and what they are saying. Your students need to know that:

Responding means letting your learners know verbally that you understand the things they tell and show you about themselves; you respond by directly communicating that you understand <u>what</u> the learners feel and <u>why</u> they feel the way they do; and responding to learners helps them to explore themselves and the lesson so they can maximize their learning.

Have 1-2 of your best students demonstrate attending behaviors in the classroom - attending physically, observing and listening. Other students should critique the demonstration, noting any steps that are left out in performing the skills.

Help your students relate their past experiences with teacher responsiveness in the classroom to today's lesson. Discuss common experiences such as:

Struggling to explain to a teacher why you are having difficulty with the assignment. The teacher asks a lot of questions but they just make you more frustrated because the questions don't deal with your problem. You finally give up and stalk off to try to finish it by yourself.

Excited, you rush to tell the teacher what happened last night. She listens very attentively and then says "That's nice. Now let's start class." She doesn't even comment on the fact that you were so happy and excited about what happened!

Help your students to describe experiences they have had where a teacher's responsiveness to them has increased their learning. For example:

As you worked on an art project, the teacher talked to you about your pleasure with it and helped you to decide that you wanted to work towards a career in art.

You will always remember that 4th grade teacher who spent time with you discussing your interests and concerns.  And it was the best year of school you ever had -- straight A's and B's!

Use an overhead or the chalkboard to show your students the following diagram.

## INTERPERSONAL SKILLS IN THE CLASSROOM

**Teacher:** ATTENDING  RESPONDING

**Learner:** Exploring

*"If we respond effectively to our learners, then they can explore themselves so that they are ready to work effectively and achieve their learning goals."*

# CHAPTER 4: RESPONDING TO FEELING
## (Pages 93-113)

## OUTLINE OF SUGGESTED TEACHING CHRONOLOGY

1. Have students take pre-test.
2. Relate attending skills to responding to feeling.
3. Relate skill of responding to feeling to previous student experiences.
4. Demonstrate and describe how to perform the skills.
5. Expand student feeling-word repertoire.
6. Role-play responding to feeling in the classroom.
7. Do small-group practice.
8. Outline applications of the skill of responding to feeling in the student's life.
9. Summarize the critical components of responding to feeling.
10. Assign homework.
11. Discuss pre-test.
12. Conduct post-test.
13. Provide feedback to reinforce growth.

1.    Tell your students to turn to page 88 and follow the instructions given in the second column. After all students have finished the task, have them rate the responses on page 89 from 1.0 (very ineffective) to 5.0 (extremely effective) with 3.0 being minimally effective.

2a.    Ask a student to role-play a learner and bring a problem to you as teacher. Attend physically, observe and listen as the "learner" talks. Then respond with an impersonal statement such as "Gee, that's too bad" or "What a shame!" Your goal should be to express <u>sympathy</u>, not <u>empathy</u>. Then have the "learner" present another problem. This time, respond to the learner's feelings using the format "You feel _____." Thus you might respond "You feel <u>confused</u>."

2b.    Discuss the two ways of responding with your students. Which would be more helpful? Which teacher would they be more likely to seek assistance from? How would they, as learners, experience each type of response?

3.    Discuss experiences students have had as teachers or learners that relate to responding to feeling.

## SAMPLE

"You complained to a teacher that you were very worried and he just told you not to feel that way. But all that did was make you more anxious about the exam."

## SAMPLE

"When you were mad at your best friend, you didn't feel good at all. And no one helped you understand the anger. The teacher just tried to get you to make up."

## SAMPLE

"When women's lib issues were discussed you always tried to make a point but no one seemed to understand."

## SAMPLE

"Everyone in your school seemed to go to Mrs. B. to talk about problems.  Somehow, the way she always talked about how you felt gave you more confidence.  It helped to talk to her about how worried you were over algebra or how disgusted you were with your role in the class play.  You always felt you had a better handle on the world after discussions with her."

4a.  With students, develop a list of the effective components of responding to feeling.  Be sure to include those in Figure 4-1.

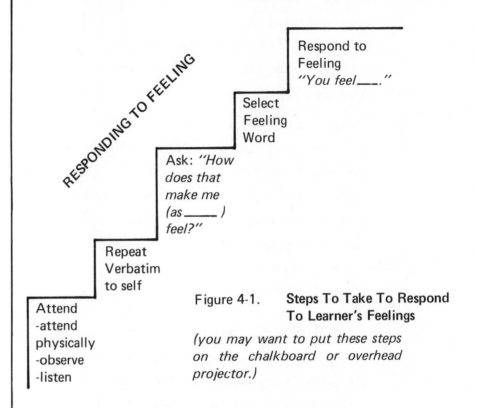

Figure 4-1.    **Steps To Take To Respond To Learner's Feelings**

*(you may want to put these steps on the chalkboard or overhead projector.)*

b.  Tell students that a feeling word relates directly to feelings. Study the first column on page 93 as an illustration of feeling words. Have students look at the learner pictured on page 94; then read your students the learner statement given on that page. Have students repeat it verbatim in their own heads and ask themselves "How does that make me (as the learner) feel?" They should write the feeling word they select using the response format "You feel_____."

c. Ask 3-4 students to read their reponses out loud. Several feeling words can accurately respond to how the learner might feel. You might compare the feelings your students selected to those given on page 97 as a response to the learner, Paul.

Students may object to the "You feel" format; "It is too rigid!" Respond to their experience of awkwardness with this new focus on responding to feeling. The most effective way to insure that beginning students in interpersonal skills respond to feeling is to use the format. This type of response will be quite helpful to their learners. As your students gain

experience in responding to feeling, they may find they can develop several alternative formats. For example: "You must feel _____," "It's got you feeling _____."

5a. Tell students that feeling words must be interchangeable with the learner's expression if they want to help the learner explore herself. Accuracy can be increased by selecting feeling words that correspond to the learner's category of feeling and the intensity of feeling. The class should look at page 100.

b. Have students turn to page 108 and identify 3 feeling words in each category of feelings by each intensity level. You may want to do this on the board as a class project.

6a. Have students do practice exercises 1-10 on page 111-112. They should concentrate on choosing

feeling words from the feeling
category and intensity level that
best suits the learner's expression.

> Encourage students to develop
> "gut" feeling words that will
> be more meaningful to learn-
> ers than extremely intellec-
> tual words.

b.  After all students have finished,
ask them to share their responses
and give one another feedback.
Feedback should focus on the accuracy of category and intensity.

c.  Your students can check themselves
out by asking "Would the learner
think that my feeling word accurately captures his or her real feeling?"

d.  Pair students in dyads.  Have them
role-play teacher/learner interactions.  The "teacher" should respond to the "learner's" feeling
using the form of "You feel_____."

> Practicing responding to
> feeling is probably one of

> the most difficult stages of
> learning for your students.
> If students are having dif-
> ficulty developing inter-
> changeable responses to
> feeling, review the steps of
> attending physically, ob-
> serving and listening.
> Students who use the attend-
> ing skills will be more
> successful than students who
> do not.  Students should keep
> their responses simple.
> Short responses to feeling
> are most helpful to learners.
> Watch out for responses such
> as "You feel <u>that</u> you're
> picked on."  "You feel <u>that</u>
> _____" responds to an
> event - "Picked on" - rather
> than a feeling -"Hurt."
> Remind students to respond <u>to</u>
> the learner, not at the
> learner.

e.  Demonstrate responding to feeling
in the classroom by having
several students role-play

learners and make statements. Use the steps of responding to feeling and respond directly to each "learner" using the format "You feel_____." Demonstrate responding to group feelings as well as individual feelings.

7. Break the class into several small groups (4-6 members). Ask students to prepare demonstrations of responding to feeling in order to aid learners in exploring themselves and their learning. Each student should have a chance to practice as "teacher." Have 1-2 groups make presentations to the whole class. Groups can rate accuracy of feeling category and intensity of the selected word.

8. Have students think of one person to whose feelings they can respond. Each student should write a list of how to respond to that person's feelings. Discuss the implications of responding to people in other areas besides the classroom.

For Example:   "Respond to my best friend.

How:    1.  Square, make eye contact.
2.  Observe her face and body.
3.  Listen to what she says.
4.  Select a feeling category.
5.  Select a feeling intensity.
6.  Respond: 'Sue, you sound like you feel_____'."

9a. Tell your students that responding to feeling sets the stage for responding to the reason for the feeling.

"IF YOU RESPOND TO THE LEARNER'S FEELING AND THE REASON FOR THE FEELING, YOUR LEARNERS WILL BE BETTER ABLE TO EXPLORE THEMSELVES AND WHY THEY FEEL THE WAY THEY DO.

b. You can have students summarize the skill of responding to feeling by having them fill in the following summary form using pages 93-113.

# RESPONDING TO FEELING - SUMMARY

| | |
|---|---|
| What is it? | (Verbally communicating understanding of learner's feelings.) |
| What does it do? | (Lets the learners know you understand where they are at.) |
| Why do it? | 1. Helps learners explore themselves.<br>2. Helps you understand the learners. |
| How do you do it? | (1. Attend physically - observe - listen.<br>2. Repeat verbatim to self.<br>3. Ask: "How does that make me (as the learner) feel."<br>4. Select feeling word.<br>5. Respond to feeling.) |
| When/Where do you do it? | (When you want to help your learners explore themselves.) |
| How do you know if you've done it right? | (How did the learner use my response?) |

10. <u>Possible</u> <u>homework</u> <u>assignments</u>:

a. Visit 2-3 classes and observe and listen for approximately 10 minutes. Record 3 responses you could make to individual learners or to the group feeling.

b. Read 93-113.

11,
12. Have students review the responses they made to the learners on page 88 when the lesson began. Now ask them to rewrite their responses to the learners. Then have them re-rate the responses on page 88.

13. Discuss the improvement in the students' responses. What implications do the changes in their responding have for their learners? What are the implications of responding to the feelings of learners who are different from themselves (racially, sexually, culturally, religiously)?

"IF I RESPOND TO MY LEARNERS' FEELINGS, THEY WILL BE BETTER ABLE TO EXPLORE THEMSELVES AND LEARN IN MY CLASSES."

# CHAPTER 4:  RESPONDING TO MEANING
### (Pages 114-118)

## OUTLINE OF SUGGESTED TEACHING CHRONOLOGY

1. Review post-test from responding to feeling.

2. Help students relate skill of responding to meaning to personal experiences.

3. Demonstrate and describe how to perform the skill.

4. Role-play responding to meaning in the classroom.

5. Do small-group practice.

6. Discuss applications of the skill of responding to meaning in each student's life.

7. Summarize the critical components of responding to meaning.

8. Assign homework.

9. Discuss post-test from responding to feelings.

10. Conduct post-test on responding to meaning.

11. Provide student feedback.

CARNEGIE LIBRARY
LIVINGSTONE COLLEGE
SALISBURY, N. C. 28144

# RESPONDING TO MEANING

1. Have students review the post-test from responding to feeling. What has improved in their responding? What is incomplete about a response to feeling only?

2. Discuss common positive and negative experiences relating to teacher's responses to meaning.

## SAMPLE

"No matter how you said it, the teacher kept misunderstanding what you said. She kept saying that your point was wrong even though you knew she thought you were making a completely different point."

3a. Develop a list of the effective components of responding to meaning (See Figure 4-2). Tell students that responding to meaning builds on the skill of responding to feeling. Be sure to include these (you may want to put them on the chalkboard).

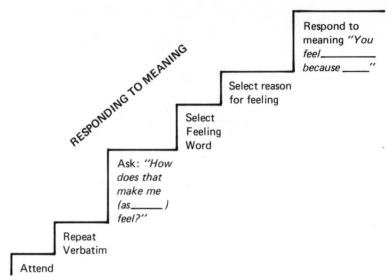

Figure 4-2. **Steps To Take To Respond To Meaning With Learners**

b. Read the examples of responses to feeling and meaning on page 114. Point out that meaning is more than just a repetition of the words the learner used.

Students often find themselves "parroting" the learner's words. This is not helpful. They should focus on meaning responses that are a short summary of what the feeling and content mean for learner. The shorter their responses

are, the better they are
likely to be.

c.  Have students look at the picture on page 115 while you read aloud the learner statement on that page.  Students should write a response to the learner's feeling and meaning using the steps for responding and the format "You feel_____ because _____."  Share alternative responses.

d.  Study the rating scale discussed on page 91.  Ask students to rate their responses using this scale.  Check one another's ratings.  You may wish to summarize the scale on the chalkboard.

### Rating Responses

3.0  Feeling and Meaning correct
2.5  Feeling only
2.0  Content only
1.5  Guidance response, no
       feeling or meaning

Students who have difficulty making accurate responses to feeling and meaning should review the skills of attending physically, observing, listening and responding to feeling.

Communicating understanding is most important.  Students may feel concerned that responding implies agreement or disagreement with the learners.  Agreement or disagreement is irrelevant until the learner knows she is understood.

### Audio-Visual Option

Show a 5-minute audio-visual tape of a teacher moving about a classroom, stopping by individual learners' desks and responding to their feeling and meaning as they talk.

### For Example:

Learner 1:  "Mrs. Brown, I got my map all finished.  But I don't know if it's right - is that

54

where Kansas goes?"

Teacher: "You feel unsure because your map might
be mixed up. Let's
see...Kansas is right."

4. Pair students in dyads to role-
play teacher/learner interactions.
"Teachers" should respond to the
feeling and meaning of their
"learners." Tell students to
give each other feedback on
whether the responses accurately
capture their feeling and meaning. Use the rating scale.

If your students are struggling
with the "You feel _____
because _____" format,
you should respond to their
discomfort and awkwardness in
mastering this new skill. As
they gain experience, they can
develop alternate formats that
are equally effective. Keep
in mind that the important
thing is to respond with an
accurate feeling word and the
reason for that feeling. Ini-

tially, however, the format
will help them focus their
attention on these two key
ingredients.

Audio-Visual Option

Show 5-10 minutes of a classroom
interaction containing approximately 10 learner/teacher interactions. In half of the interactions the teacher should respond to the learners using the
form "You feel _____ because
_____." In half of the inter-
actions the teacher should not
respond to the learners' feeling
and meaning.

Have students identify which
teacher statements were responsive
and would help the learners
explore and increase learning and
which teacher statements were not
responsive.

5a. Demonstrate responding in the
classroom to your students. Have
them role-play learners involved
in some task (e.g., history
project -building a textile map.)
Respond to individuals and the

group using the format "You feel_____ because _____."

b.  With your students, you may wish to think of situations and possible responses that a teacher might use with groups of learners. Common group responses might be:

"You feel proud because you all passed the exam."  "You feel mixed up because this science experiment did not work according to the theory in the book." "You feel sad because Johnny is our friend and we'll miss him when he moves."

c.  Ask several students to role-play the teacher and respond to the class while the other students role-play learners.  Have the class critique their work by attending, observing and listening to the reaction of the "learners" to the "teacher's" responses.

Break the class into several small groups (4-6 members).  Have each group prepare and practice a demonstration of responding during different classes (e.g., reading, psychology, math, gym). Each student should practice responding to learners.

d.  Have 1-2 groups demonstrate for the whole class.  Other students should write alternative responses the "teacher" could have made as well as rate the accuracy of the "teacher's" response.

6a.  As a group, identify other applications for the skills of responding besides the classroom. Complete the chart below.  (See Figure 4-3.)  You may want to work on an overhead or the chalkboard.

| | At Home | At School | At Work | In The Community |
|---|---|---|---|---|
| Other people and Situations | | | | |

Figure 4-3. **Applications for responding skills**

b. discuss the possible effects of responding in the other situations.

7a. Summarize the skill of responding to meaning.

"IF YOU RESPOND ACCURATELY TO THE FEELING AND MEANING OF YOUR LEARNERS, YOU WILL LET THE LEARN-ERS KNOW YOU UNDERSTAND THEM AND YOU WILL BE A MORE EFFECTIVE TEACHER."

Have students complete the following summary form using pages 114-118.

> Help students to understand that the final aim is learning! By using interpersonal skills, the teacher is more effective in maintaining the discipline and exploration that creates the best conditions for learning. Learners of teachers who respond do well in the classroom.

8. Possible Homework Assignments

a. Visit a classroom and observe for 10-15 minutes. For every learner statement, write a response to feeling and meaning. Write a response to the group.

b. If your students are presently student-teaching in any capacity, they should:

1) respond to each of their learners each week;

2) respond to the entire group once each day; and

3) record an evaluation of their responding behavior at the end of each day.

c. Read pages 114-118.

9, Have students read the responses
10. they made in the post-test for responding to feeling. Have them re-write their responses. Then have them complete the post-test on pages 120-121.

11. Discuss with students the in-creased accuracy of their re-sponses to their learners and their ability to help the learn-ers explore themselves and the learning material.

# RESPONDING TO MEANING - SUMMARY

**What is it?**

(Summarizing the reason for learner's feeling.)

**What does it do?**

(Helps the learners explore where they are in relation to themselves and the lesson.)

**Why do it?**

(Lets learner know the teacher understands him or her. Cannot effectively teach without this minimum response.)

**How do you do it?**

1. Attend - physically attend, observe, listen.

2. Repeat verbatim to yourself.

3. Ask: "How does that make me (as the learner) feel?"

4. Select feeling word.

5. Select reason for feeling.

6. Respond to meaning - "You feel _____ because _____ .")

**When/Where do you do it?**

(In the classroom - with individuals and with groups of learners.)

**How do you know if you've done it right?**

("Do my learners acknowledge my response - go on to talk more about themselves and their relation to themselves, to me or to the learning material?" Use attending skills.)

# CHAPTER 4: SUMMARY OF RESPONDING

1. Review the major points of the skill of responding. Include these points:

a. Responding to learner's feeling and meaning lets them know you understand where they are coming from.

b. Responding to learners helps them explore themselves and their relation to you and to the learning materials.

c. Responding to learners makes them more open to you and increases their learning in the classroom.

d. Responding to the learner puts you in control.

### Audio-Visual Option

Show three 5-minute audio-visual segments of 3 different teachers interacting with learners. Ask students to rate each teacher on her attending and responding behaviors. Students should support their ratings by listing what behaviors the teachers did and did not do. Discuss the ratings for each teacher. Break students into small groups. Each group can practice attending and responding to learners who are involved in learning tasks. Students should rate each other and support their ratings.

1) Develop alternative uses for th attending and responding skills. Have each student list a person they could use the attending and responding behavior with. Students should write a list of how to attend and respond to that person.

2) Pair students in dyads. Have students role-play the alternatives developed above to provide students with additional practice.

Summarize the behaviors studied so far and the relationship between the behaviors. You may want to put this diagram on the chalkboard or an overhead projector.

**CLASSROOM INTERPERSONAL SKILLS**

Teacher: ATTEND ▶ RESPOND

◇

Learner:                    EXPLORE

*"If you can attend and respond to learners so that you can enter the learner's frame of reference and relate the learning material to that frame of reference, you are beginning to teach effectively."*

2.    Possible Homework Assignments

a.    Review pages 86-125.

b.    Have students practice attending and responding in their class-rooms.  They should attend to each learner once each day (primary grades)  or once each week (secondary grades.)  They should respond to each learner in cycles, making sure to respond to 10-15 learners each day.  Have them record and rate their use of interpersonal skills in the classroom.

c.    If students are involved in other teaching courses where they must make presentations, have them use the interpersonal skills of attending and responding there as well.

d.    When possible, visit students in their classrooms and provide them with feedback on their use of attending and responding with their learners.

# UNIT 5:  PERSONALIZING SKILLS

Concept:      <u>Personalizing</u> - the act of relating the learners' frames of reference to learning goals.

Principle:    <u>If</u> the teachers relate the learners' frames of reference to learning goals, <u>then</u> the learners will know where they are in relation to where they want to be <u>so</u> <u>that</u> the teacher will be able to help the learners take the steps to get to the learning goal.

Skills Objective:    Learning the skills that make up personalizing skills.

**OBJECTIVE**
**PERSONALIZING SKILLS**

**PERSONALIZING GOALS:** *personalizing the learners' behavioral goals (pp 140-146)*

Reflecting behavioral goals
Formulating behavioral goals
Discovering behavioral goals

**PERSONALIZING PROBLEMS:** *personalizing the learners' behavioral deficits (pp 137-139)*

Reflecting behavioral deficits
Formulating behavioral deficits

**Skills Program:** *Steps*   Discovering behavioral deficits

**PERSONALIZING MEANING:** *personalizing the learners' responsibility for behavior (pp 130-136)*

Reflecting personal responsibility
Externalizing the reason
Building a responsive base

# CHAPTER 5: PERSONALIZING SKILLS
## (Pages 125-151)

## PRELIMINARY POINTS

Personalizing is simply helping your learners gain direction in their learning experiences by helping them understand where they are in relation to where they want or need to be in the lesson.

Your students need to know the following:

Personalizing is a verbal response to where the learner is now and where she is going.

You personalize by using your own experience to understand the learner at deeper levels than she has expressed.

Personalizing helps the learners to understand themselves so they can gain direction in their learning experiences.

## STIMULUS SUGGESTIONS

Have 1-2 of your best students demonstrate attending and responding behavior in the classroom. Other students should critique the demonstrations, noting any steps that are left out in performing the skills.

Remind the class that attending behaviors prepare you to teach while responding behaviors let you communicate understanding to your learners of where they are. Both skills prepare you to personalize with your learners to help them understand their own experiences in terms of where they are at and where they are going.

Show your students the following diagram (See Figure 5-1). You may want to put it on the chalkboard or an overhead.

**Teacher:** ATTENDING ▶ RESPONDING    PERSONALIZING

**Learner:**                    EXPLORING    UNDERSTANDING

Figure 5-1.    **Classroom interpersonal skills**

Help students relate personalizing to their past experiences through

62 discussing common experiences they've had as teachers or learners in classroom.

## SAMPLE

"The guidance counselor calls you in to talk about your low grades. Even though you know you are at least partially to blame, you complain about the teachers while she talks and talks about your poor attendance record. Finally you just give up and wait for her to finish so you can go back to what you were doing before you got called in.

Show your students Figure 5-2 (You may want to have mimeographed copies to hand out to your students.)

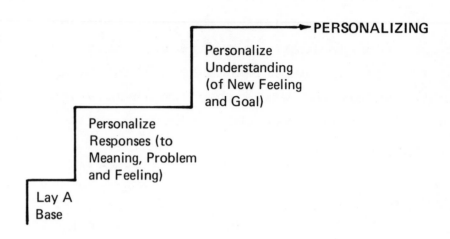

Figure 5-2. **The steps of personalizing**

# CHAPTER 5:  LAYING A BASE
### (Pages 131-135)

## OUTLINE OF SUGGESTED TEACHING CHRONOLOGY

1. Have students relate the skill of laying a base to their present experience.
2. Review interpersonal skills previously studied.
3. Preview skill of laying a base.
4. Demonstrate and show how to perform the skill.
5. Role-play laying a base with a learner.
6. Do small-group practices.
7. Discuss applications of the skill of laying a base to the students' lives.
8. Summarize the critical components of the skill of laying a base.
9. Conduct post-test.
10. Provide feedback to reinforce learning and growth.

# LAYING A BASE

1. Tell students to write a brief paragraph describing what they would do as teachers if a learner came to them complaining of the difficulty she or he had with a social studies research assignment.

2. After all students have finished writing, ask 2 students to role-play the situation for the class. Discuss with students what was good about the demonstration, focusing on the use of attending and responding. You might ask:

   a. "What have we learned that you saw being used in the demonstration?"

   b. "What did the teacher do correctly to help the learner explore?"

3. Discuss with students how the "teacher" in the demonstration might have been more effective in helping the learner. Encourage students to explore how the skills of attending and responding might have been more effectively utlized.

FOR EXAMPLE

The demonstrating "teacher" may have very quickly told the learner to go to the encyclopedia, but the learner may have already done that. The teacher could have spent more time responding to the learner so that she knew what the learner had done already.

4a. Read the teacher/learner exchange on page 132 to students. Have them identify which skill (responding to feeling and meaning) the teacher is using.

b. Your students need to know the following things about laying a base:

It is the process of making a <u>series</u> of feeling and meaning responses to learners.

It helps you to explore fully with the learners so you will know where they are at and can be more "on top" of your learners.

c.   Develop a list of the effective ingredients of laying a base.  Be sure to include these (you may want to put Figure 5-3 on the chalkboard):

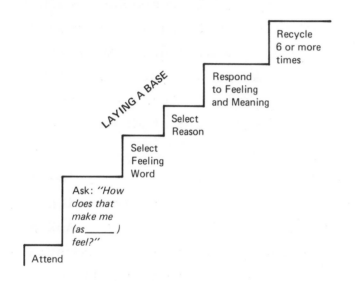

Figure 5-3.   **Steps To Take In Laying A Base**

5a: Have students write their own responses to Paul on page 131. Students should share and rate the responses they write, using the scale given on page 123.

b.   Assign one student to read the learner statements on page 133.

The other students should formulate responses to feeling and meaning in their heads.  After each learner statement, call on one student to respond verbally to the "learner" while other students rate the response. Discuss ratings and alternative responses only after all of the learner statements have been responded to.

c.   Group students in triads to role-play teacher/learner interchanges of at least 3 responses (see Figure 5-4).  The third student should rate the responses and provide feedback.

| "Learner" | "Teacher" | "Rater" |
|---|---|---|
| Share 2-3 Sentences | Respond to feeling & meaning | Rate response |
| Explore using teacher's responses | Respond to feeling and meaning | Rate response |
| Explore | Respond | Rate response |
| Explore | | |
| Give feedback to "teacher" | Evaluate own responses | Give Ratings and Feedback |

Figure 5-4. **Role-playing exercise for laying a base**

66

Student feedback on responses should use the rating scale and the "learners" reaction. A response can be technically correct; but if it does not further the learner's exploration, it is not a helpful response.

d.  Have students exchange roles and repeat exercise until all students have been "teacher," "learner" and "rater." Once all students can effectively respond 3 times in a row, you may wish to have them practice responding 6 times.

Laying an effective base with their learners in the classroom will usually require that students be able to respond at least 6-9 times. With some learners and some situations, they will need to be able to respond as many as 50 times. The better the base laid, the more students will be able to help identify and solve learners problems later!

As students practice laying a base, float around the room and help them to keep their responses accurate. If their responses begin to get off track, you should help students review the steps of interpersonal skills. Using the steps will help students respond accurately.

6a.  Select 3-4 students to role-play learners during a discussion about an upcoming test. Ask a student volunteer to demonstrate a "teacher" who responds to individual learners and to the group during the discussion.

FOR EXAMPLE

Learner 1:  "Yech! I don't want to take a math test."

Teacher:  "You feel bad because the test might be hard to pass."

Learner 2: "This stuff we've been studying is really hard."

Teacher: "You feel worried because the material is difficult to learn."

Learner 3: "It just doesn't make any sense to me. I don't know how to do it."

Teacher: "You feel lost because it hasn't fallen together for you."

Learner 2: "Why can't we study it some more before we have a test."

Teacher: "You feel scared because a test would be impossible to do well on with what you know now."

Have the rest of the class rate the "teacher" and write alternative responses to the learners.

b. Group students in small groups (3-4 members). Have each group write a short script illustrating responding during a teacher/learner discussion using different activities and subjects (e.g., science lab, health class discussion.) After all groups are finished, have 1-2 groups role-play their script while the rest of the class rates the responses.

7a. Divide class into 3 larger groups. Have each group list 3 non-teaching situations where laying a base would be effective to use and give 2 reasons for laying a base in each situation. One group can work on home situations, one on work situations and one on community situations.

Ask each group to share their applications of laying a base with the whole class. You might have one student from each group list the situations and reasons on the chalkboard.

Students may worry about losing old responses that they have found effective with learners in the past. Encourage them to ADD this

68

new responding skill to their repertoire - they won't lose anything!

8a. Tell your students that laying a base is one of the personalizing skills that help you to effectively teach learners.

"IF YOU LAY A BASE WITH YOUR LEARNERS, YOU WILL BE ON TOP OF WHERE THEY ARE AT SO THAT YOU CAN GUIDE THEIR LEARNING MORE EFFECTIVELY."

b. Have students summarize the skill of laying a base, using the form on the next page and pages 131-135. You might synthesize their efforts into one master summary on the chalkboard or an overhead projector.

9, Tell students to write a brief

10a. paragraph describing what they would do if 3-4 learners came to them to discuss their improved ability or their failure to improve in ability to use a skill such as attending.

b. Ask 2-3 students to discuss their ability to lay a base with learners and the implications for their future teaching while another role-plays the teacher who helps them discuss their ability. Have the rest of the class rate the "teacher's responses.

11. Discuss with the students what was good about the demonstration. Ask them to compare the "teacher's responsiveness to the responsiveness of the "teacher" who gave the demonstration with which class began. You might ask: "Which 'teacher' learned more about the learner?" or "Which 'teacher' would you be more likely to listen to and take directions from?"

# LAYING A BASE - SUMMARY

| | |
|---|---|
| What <u>is</u> <u>it?</u> | (A series of feeling and meaning responses to a learner.) |
| What <u>does</u> <u>it</u> <u>do?</u> | (Helps learners to fully explore where they are.) |
| Why <u>do</u> <u>it?</u> | (Builds a base of understanding. Increases the effectiveness of later direction that you give to your learners.) |
| How <u>do</u> <u>you</u> <u>do</u> <u>it?</u> | (1. Attend. <br><br> 2. Ask: "How does that make me (as _____ ) feel?" <br><br> 3. Select feeling word. <br><br> 4. Select reason for feeling. <br><br> 5. Respond to feeling and meaning. <br><br> 6. Recycle 6 or more times.) |
| When/Where <u>do</u> <u>it?</u> | (In the classroom when you want to help a learner establish direction.) |
| How <u>do</u> <u>you</u> <u>know</u> <u>if</u> <u>you've</u> <u>done it right?</u> | (If your learner continues to use what you say to explore herself or her relation to the world and the learning material.) |

CHAPTER 5: PERSONALIZING RESPONSES
(Pages 135-139)


## OUTLINE OF SUGGESTED TEACHING CHRONOLOGY

1. Have students relate skill of personalizing responses to previous experiences.

2. Have students review preceding skills.

3. Have students take pre-test.

4. Demonstrate and describe steps of how to perform the skill.

5. Role-play personalizing responses in the classroom.

6. Do small group practice of personalizing responses with learners.

7. Apply the skill of personalizing responses to the students' lives.

8. Summarize the critical components of personalizing responses.

9. Assign homework.

10. Discuss pre-test.

11. Conduct post-test.

12. Provide feedback to reinforce growth.

## PERSONALIZING RESPONSES

1. Discuss common experiences students have had where teachers have tried to convince them that they were practically or fully responsible for something.

### SAMPLE

"The morning before your science project was due, you panicked and went to talk to the teacher because you weren't done yet. The teacher earnestly said it was too bad you couldn't work with deadlines; you got annoyed, and left. And it's still true! You never meet deadlines."

### SAMPLE

"The principal threatened to suspend you because you got caught smoking on the school bus. And in the process he told you lots of things you did wrong and goofed up. You always disliked him afterwards."

2a. Discuss with your students how the teacher or adult in these kinds of experiences might have been more effective in helping them change their behavior in school. Specifically, help your students understand that attending and responding behaviors could have increased their openess to listening to and using the input.

b. Discuss the need to give learners direction in more constructive ways than teachers often do. Point out to the students that personalizing responses will give them a way to prepare to give direction that the learners will be open to.

3. Have students write their best response to the learner expression given on page 127. Have students rate the responses given on page 128. Ask them to compare their ratings to the expert ratings on page 129. You might get a show of hands to find out how many rated the responses the same as the experts.

72

4a. Define personalized responses with
your students. Ask them to identify as many reasons for personalizing responses as they can. (You
may want to list the reasons on
the chalkboard.) Be sure your
learners know that personalized
responses do the following:

Involve the learners directly by
focusing on their role in their
experiences.
Require a base of understanding
built through attending, responding
and laying a base with learners.
Help learners increase their level
of self-responsibility and decrease
their irresponsibility.

b. Develop a list of the effective
ingredients of personalized responses with your students. Be
sure to include these (you may
want to put Figure 5-5 on the
chalkboard or an overhead projector):

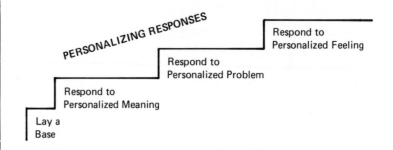

Figure 5-5.    Steps To Take In Personalizing Responses

c. Tell your students that the first
step in personalizing responses is
to personalize meaning. You
personalize by asking yourself
"What is the learner's role in the
experience?" or "How is the
learner involved in causing the
problem?" The best way to personalize meaning is to use the form
"You feel_____ because you
_____."

d. Show students the responses on
page 136. Ask them to identify

which is a response to feeling and meaning. Which is a response to personalized meaning? What is the difference between the two responses?

e.  Ask students to write a response to personalized meaning for the learner statement on page 127. They should use the form "You feel _____ because you _____." Have 2-3 students read their responses.

> The learner's role in the experience may be a past role, a present role or a future role.

f.  Tell your students that the second step in personalized responses is to personalize the problem. You personalize by asking "What is it the learner cannot do that creates this experience for her?" The best way to personalize this deficit is to use the form "You feel_____ because you cannot _____."

g.  Show students the response to the personalized problem in the first column on page 137. Ask them to notice the difference between this response and a response to personalized meaning.

h.  Ask students to write a response to the personalized problem for the learner statement on page 127. They should use the form "You feel_____ because you cannot _____." Have 2-3 students read their responses.

> Personalized problems are behavioral. Students should check their personalized problem to be sure it identifies a behavior that the learner lacks which contributes to the problem. The purpose is to help the learner assume responsibility, not to assess blame or fault. If the learners can assume responsibility, then they can choose to handle the existing environment, change

74

the environment or find a
new environment.

i. Tell your students that the third
step in personalized responses is
to personalize the feeling. You
personalize the feeling by asking
"How does this deficit make the
learner feel about him/herself?"
The best way to personalize the
feeling is to use the format "You
feel_____ because you cannot
_____."

j. Show students the response to
personalized feeling in the
second column on page 137. Ask
them to notice the implications
of the new feeling word.

k. Ask students to write a response
to personalized feeling for the
learner statement on page 127.
They should use the form "You
feel_____ because you cannot
_____." Have 2-3 students read
their responses.

5a. Have your students re-write their
responses to Mary on page 133.

They should write 2 responses to
Mary's feeling and meaning in
order to lay a base. Then have
them write 1 response to personalize the meaning, 1 to personalize the problem and 1 to personalize the feeling.

b. Ask various students to read the
response they feel is their best.
The rest of the class can rate
the responses using the scale
given on page 129.

c. Pair students. Have each dyad
write 5 learner statements.
Exchange learner statements between dyads and have each dyad
write 3 responses to each learner
statement as follows:

1) "You feel_____ because you_____."
2) "You feel_____ because you cannot_____."
3) "You feel_____ because you cannot_____."

Return the learner statements and
responses to the dyad that wrote
the learner statements. Have
them rate the responses using the
scale on page 129.

Audio-Visual Option

Show three 5-minute excerpts of teacher/learner interactions. Ask students to rate the teacher responses. Have students write the best response they could make to the learner. Share ratings and alternative responses.

d. Group students in triads. Have 2 students in each triad role-play a teacher/learner interaction while the third student rates the interaction. The "teacher" should personalize responses following the steps given in 4b. Students should give the "teacher" feedback. Then students should change roles until each student has been "teacher."

Personalizing must be based on a number of accurate responses. Students may wish to make several responses to personalize meaning before personalizing the problem and feeling. They may also return to responding to feeling and meaning after personalizing the meaning, problem or feeling.

In order to personalize responses that will help the learners accept responsibility for themselves, the steps must be followed in order. Your students may tend to skip ahead to the problem before having laid a base. Be sure they lay a base of at least 6-9 responses to feeling and meaning first. Then they should personalize the meaning - then the problem - and then the feeling.

6a. Discuss the use of personalizing responses with groups of learners as well as with individuals. As a group, list situations where a teacher might be able to personalize with a group of learners.

FOR EXAMPLE:

1. Gym class - exploring why one team always loses.

2. English - knowing how to make a speech.

3. Social science - deciding on career goals.

4. Science - with a group of minority students.

b. Divide the class in half. Ask each group to select one of the situations listed in 6a and write a script to role-play the scene with the use of personalized responses. Have each group demonstrate its scene to the other group.

Learner acceptance of responses is not a green light to continued personalizing and initiating. It is necessary but not sufficient. The responses must be <u>accurate</u> as well.

Audio-Visual Option

Record each demonstration on audiovisual tape for possible use in later classes.

7. Ask students to list other non-teaching situations where personalized responses would be useful to them. Discuss the implications of personalizing responses in these situatuions.

8. Summarize personalized responding with your class. Have students write a summary using the form on the next page. Ask students to share their summaries as a way of checking out their understanding. "IF YOU PERSONALIZE YOUR RESPONSES TO YOUR STUDENTS, THEY WILL LEARN TO ACCEPT MORE PERSONAL RESPONSIBILITY FOR THEIR BEHAVIOR IN YOUR CLASSROOM."

9. <u>Possible Homework Assignments</u>:

a. Ask students to visit 2 classrooms and record the number of personalized responses they hear. They should write their own responses where they felt one was needed.

b. Pair students for outside assignments. Each student should explore some difficulty she has as a learner while the other student responds. Both students should rate the responses and write a summary of the interchange.

# PERSONALIZING RESPONSES - SUMMARY

**What is it?** (Involving the learners directly in their expression of their experience. Focusing on the learner.)

**What does it do?** (Makes the learners responsible for their experiences and for themselves.)

**Why do it?**
1. Provides you with a means for going beyond what the learners express.
2. Identifies what the learner cannot do.
3. Helps the learner assume control of himself.

**How do you do it?**
1. Lay a base.
2. Respond to personalized meaning.
3. Respond to personalized problem.
4. Respond to personalized feeling.

**When/Where do you do it?** (In the classroom when learners need to be prepared for personalizing goals.)

**How do you know you've done it right?** (By your learners' reaction - they can use what you are saying by continuing to explore.)

10,  Recall with students how many

11.  rated the responses on page 128 the same as the experts. Have students re-write their response to the learner on page 127 to make their best response. Ask them to re-rate the responses on page 128.

12.  Have students rate their original response and their new response to the learner on page 127. Ask your students several questions relating to their improved ability to personalize responses. You might ask:

"How many rated your second response to the learner higher than your first?"

"How many rated more responses the same as the expert?"
"In what way could you help a learner identify a problem, that you could not do before?"

# CHAPTER 5: PERSONALIZING UNDERSTANDING
### (Pages 140-145)

## OUTLINE OF SUGGESTED TEACHING CHRONOLOGY

1. Relate personalizing understanding to students' experience.

2. Relate demonstration to previous skills studied.

3. Review post-test from personalizing responses.

4. Demonstrate and describe how to perform the skill.

5, Role-play personalizing understanding in the classroom.

6. Do small-group practice.

7. Give applications of the skill to the students' lives.

8. Summarize the critical components of personalizing understanding.

9. Assign homework.

10. Conduct post-test for personalizing understanding.

11. Review post-test from personalizing meaning.

12. Provide feedback to reinforce growth.

1.  Show class a video-tape of a teacher/learner interaction. The teacher should use attending, responding and personalizing skills with the learner but should <u>not</u> identify any learner goal.

## SAMPLE

Learner:   "I try to get along but the kids don't like me."

Teacher:   "You feel bad because they are not your friends."

Learner:   "They never ask me to play with them."

Teacher:   "You feel hurt because they leave you alone."

Learner:   "I'm always by myself!"

Teacher:   "You feel terrible because you are alone."

Learner:   "I'd like to have friends. Why don't I?"

Teacher:   "You feel terrible because you can't make friends with anybody."

Learner:   "I guess I'll never have a friend."

Teacher:   "You feel scared because you can't make friends and you're always alone."

2.  Ask students to rate the teacher responses in the video-tape. Have them identify what they feel the teacher might want to do next. What do they think would be useful to the learner?"

3.  Have students re-read their final response to the learner on page 127 from the lesson on personalizing responses. How is it similar to the video-tape shown in step 1? What might they want to do next as a teacher?

4a. Make sure students know that:

1)  personalizing understanding responds to where the learners want to be;

2)  it establishes direction for the learners; and

3)  if you can personalize understanding, you will be ready to deal with learner problems.

b.  Develop the components of personal-
    izing understanding with the
    students.
    Be sure to include these (you may
    want to put Figure 5-6 on the
    chalkboard or an overhead pro-
    jector).

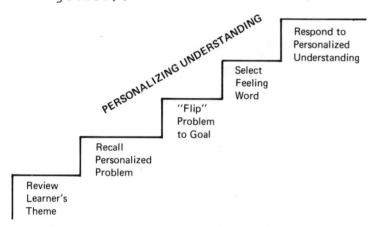

Figure 5-6.    **Steps To Take In Personalizing Understanding**

c.  Read to students the teacher/
    learner exchanges on page 141.
    Tell students that personalized
    understanding responses provide
    learner direction by identifying a
    goal where the learner wants or
    needs to be.  The best way to learn
    how to personalize understanding is
    to use the format "You feel_____

because you cannot _____ and you
want to _____."  Have students
check the teacher responses on page
141.  Do the responses identify a
learner goal?

d.  Explain to your students that there
    are several cues for identifying
    the learner's theme or overall
    program.  You might list the cues
    and see if your students can think
    of additional cues.

Cues to learner's theme

1)  Learner repeats it a lot.

2)  Learner identifies how it
    makes him or her feel.

3)  Learner is intense about it.

e.  Have your students write a person-
    alized understanding response to
    the learner on page 127.  Tell them
    to check their response by asking
    the following:

1)  Does it identify the learner's
    goal?

2)  Does it have the same pieces
    as the format  "You feel

_____ because you cannot
_____ and you want to
_____?"

5a. Have students generate as many personalized understanding responses as they can to Paul on page 131 and Mary on page 133. Check the responses.

b. Group students in triads as teacher/learner/rater. Have each triad practice personalizing understanding. Students should use the rating scale on page 129.

> To effectively personalize understanding, students will need to lay a base and personalize their responses to meaning, feeling and problem before personalizing understanding. Students should practice personalizing understanding only if they can use all preceding skills.

6a. Break class into several small groups (4-6 members). Ask each group to practice and then tape-record a possible classroom discussion, role-playing teacher and learners. The discussion should end with an effective personalized understanding response by the "teacher." Possible discussion topics: choosing a field trip destination in history class; entering a drama contest; solving a complex math problem.

Have the whole class listen to 1-2 tapes and rate each response. Share ratings and develop alternative responses.

7. Have students think of 3 areas where they can personalize understanding for themselves. Explore why students would find it useful to personalize understanding for themselves with the class.

8a. Summarize the critical components of personalizing understanding.

"IF YOU EFFECTIVELY PERSONALIZE UNDERSTANDING FOR YOUR LEARNERS, YOU WILL BE READY TO DEAL WITH THEIR LEARNING PROBLEMS SO THEY CAN

BE BETTER LEARNERS IN YOUR CLASS-ROOM."

b.  Use the following summary form to help students check their under-standing of the skill of person-alizing understanding.  You might have 2-3 students find the answer to each question using pages 140-145.  Then have students write answers on the chalkboard and answer questions other students might have about the answer.

9.  Possible Homework Assignments

a.  Have students pick one area where they might personalize understand-ing with themselves and write 5 responses to themselves:  feeling and feeling-plus meaning responses, personalized meaning, personalized problem, personalized feeling and personalized goal responses.

b.  Have students visit a classroom during a group discussion.  Write 5 responses to the group during the discussion:  feeling, feeling and meaning, personalized meaning, personalized problem, personalized feeling, personalized goal.

10.  Have students complete the post-training assessment on pages 147-148.

11.  Ask students to rate the responses they made to the learner on page 127 at the end of the personalizing responses lesson.  Ask them to rate their response to the learner on page 147.

12.  Discuss students' improved ability to provide useful direction to their learners.  You might ask: "How many of you provided goals for your learners before the lesson?"

"How many of you tied the goals to your responding skills?"
"Who could help learners in explor-ing where they are and relating it to where they need to be?"
"How does what you would do now compare to what you would have done before the lesson?"

# PERSONALIZING UNDERSTANDING – SUMMARY

| | |
|---|---|
| What <u>is</u> <u>it</u>? | (Responding to where the learners want to be.) |
| What <u>does</u> <u>it</u> <u>do</u>? | (Establishes a direction which the learners can use within their frame of reference.) |
| Why <u>do</u> <u>it</u>? | 1. Identifies where the learner wants to be. <br> 2. Helps the learner assume control of herself. <br> 3. Provides you with a means of responding to the discrepancy between where learners are and where they need or want to be. |
| How <u>do</u> <u>you</u> <u>do</u> <u>it</u>? | 1. Review learner's theme. <br> 2. Recall personalized problem. <br> 3. "Flip" problem to goal. <br> 4. Select feeling word. <br> 5. Respond to personalized understanding. |
| When/Where <u>do</u> <u>you</u> <u>do</u> <u>it</u>? | (After you and the learner understand what they cannot do.) |
| How <u>do</u> <u>you</u> <u>know</u> <u>if</u> <u>you've</u> <u>done</u> <u>it</u> <u>right</u>? | (Your learners continue to explore where they are in relation to where they want or need to be.) |

# CHAPTER 5: SUMMARY OF PERSONALIZING

1. Review the major points of personalizing. Be sure to include these points:

   Personalizing skills prepare your learners to listen to you and involve themselves in the learning material.

   Personalizing helps your learners to understand themselves at deeper levels.

   Personalizing will prepare you to effectively solve learning and discipline problems in your classroom.

2. Show students a 5-minute audio-visual tape of a teacher dealing with a difficult learner (e.g., a learner in math who is goofing off rather than working on the assigned problems). Do not have the teacher use high levels of attending, responding or personalizing skills.

3. Divide class into 3 groups. Ask each group to prepare and practice a demonstration of how the same scene might have been ideally handled by a teacher with high levels of attending, responding and personalizing skills.

4. Have 1 group demonstrate the "ideal" situation for the whole class. Other students can critique it by adding further suggestions for improvement.

5. Develop alternative uses for personalizing skills. Divide class into 3 groups. Have each group prepare a demonstration of using personalizing skill in non-teaching situations. One group can focus on a home situation, one on a work situation and one on a community situation.

For Example

Home          - a mother helping her
                child develop a
                money-earning scheme.

Work     - a teacher being
           helped to develop
           new reading curric-
           ulum.

Community - small group committee
            to select a civic
            project

6.  Summarize the skills studied so far
    and the relationship between the
    behaviors.  You may want to put
    this diagram on the chalkboard or
    an overhead projector.

**CLASSROOM INTERPERSONAL SKILLS**

Teacher:    ATTEND ▶ RESPOND    PERSONALIZE

Learner:             EXPLORE    UNDERSTAND

*"If you can personalize your
understanding of where your
learners want or need to be, you
can increase your learners' educational achievement and decrease
discipline problems."*

# UNIT 6: INITIATING SKILLS

# SUMMARY OF KEY CONCEPTS FOR CHAPTER 6

Concept: <u>Initiating</u> - the act of helping the learners take the steps to achieve the learning goals.

Principle: <u>If</u> the teacher helps the learners take the steps, <u>then</u> the learners will achieve their learning goals <u>so</u> <u>that</u> the learners will be able to learn more effectively.

Skills
Objective: Learning the skills that make up initiating skills.

**OBJECTIVE**
**INITIATING SKILLS**

**DEVELOPING SUB-STEPS** — *planning sub-steps to achieve steps (pp 172-175)*

Taking mini-steps
Developing mini-steps
Developing mini-goals

**DEVELOPING STEPS** — *planning steps to achieve goals (pp 163-171)*

Developing additional steps
Developing intermediary steps
Developing first step

**Skills Program:** *Steps*   **DEFINING GOALS** — *breaking goals out into component parts (pp 157-162)*

Answering basic questions
Asking basic questions
Breaking out personalized goal

# CHAPTER 6: INITIATING SKILLS
### (Pages 152-185)

## PRELIMINARY POINTS

Help your students relate today's lesson to their past experiences. How many have had the experiences below or similar experiences?

"Worked out an exciting special project idea in science class with a teacher yet never followed through on the idea. You still think it would have been a great project."

"Determined to get along better with a teacher; maybe even talked to the teacher about it. You tried hard but you never did get along better with the teacher. And you never did quite figure out what was going wrong."

Initiating simply means providing learners with a plan to reach their goals. Your students need to know these points:

Initiating means giving the learners a program to reach their goals.

You initiate with your learners by helping them plan a series of behaviors to get them from where they are to where they want to be.

Initiating demonstrates a willingness to share your knowledge and skills to help the learner overcome a personal problem.

Initiating with your learners helps them to act on their learning before they become discipline problems.

Effective initiating requires attending, responding and personalizing skills.

## STIMULUS SUGGESTIONS

Have students do pre-training assessment on pages 154-155. Ask students to share and rate their responses to the learner on page 154.

Discuss their responses.  How did they
formulate their responses?  What did
they use to make an effective response?
What gaps do the students feel continue
to exist in their responses?

Use an overhead or the chalkboard
to show your students Figure 6-1.

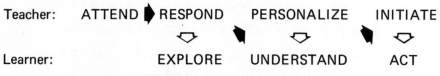

Teacher:    ATTEND ▶ RESPOND    PERSONALIZE    INITIATE

Learner:              EXPLORE    UNDERSTAND    ACT

Figure 6-1.  Classroom interpersonal skills model

*"If you initiate effectively with
your learners, you facilitate the
learners' ability to act on their
learning."*

# CHAPTER 6:  DEFINING THE GOAL
### (Pages 157-162)

## OUTLINE OF SUGGESTED TEACHING CHRONOLOGY

1.  Have students take pre-test.
2.  Relate previous skills to defining the goal.
3.  Relate defining the goal to students' previous experience.
4.  Demonstrate and describe how to perform the skill.
5.  Do large-group practice.
6.  Role-play defining goals with learners.
7.  Outline applications of the skill of defining goals to the students' lives.
8.  Summarize the critical components of defining goals.
9.  Assign homework.
10. Discuss pre-test.
11. Conduct post-test.
12. Provide feedback to reinforce growth.

## DEFINING THE GOAL

1. Ask students what steps they would take to prepare to teach a lesson on addition to a group of learners. List the steps they name on the chalkboard or an overhead projector.

2. Check (✔) the steps students list which relate to the interpersonal skills of attending, responding and personalizing (e.g., find out what the learners can or cannot already do; in addition, find out the learners' ages.) Circle the steps which relate to initiating (e.g., determining exactly what you want learners to learn to do).

3. Discuss with students some experiences they have had in classrooms that relate to defining the goal.

### SAMPLE

"Remember the social science teacher who always left you thoroughly confused? What was the point of the lesson? You could never figure out what the teacher was trying to help you learn. Nothing seemed to hang together."

### SAMPLE

"Have you ever started to research a paper and just been lost because you weren't sure what you were trying to accomplish with the paper?"

4a. Make sure your students know that defining the goal involves answering basic questions that let us know what is involved in reaching the goals. Develop a list of the basic questions that relate to defining goals. Be sure to include the questions in Figure 6-2 (see next page).

b. Show students the questions on page 157. Read the paragraph under each question and compare with the goal defined on page 159.

5b. Ask your class to do the exercise on page 161. Have 1-2 students read their answers. Have all students compare their answers to those on page 162 and add additional information if needed.

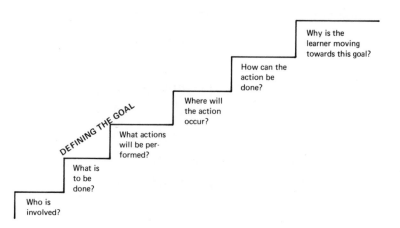

Figure 6-2. **Questions To Answer In Defining The Goals**

b. Re-read to students the teacher/learner interaction on page 134. Ask students to develop a defined goal for Mary.

c. Using the chalkboard or an overhead projector, develop the defined goal for Mary. Draw upon students' work in 5b. to do so.

6a. Pair students to role-play teacher/learner interactions. The "learner" should explore a simple problem (e. g., failed test, lab experiment she can't complete) with the help of the "teacher." Then the "teacher" and "learner" should define the goal using the six questions.

b. Have 2-3 pairs of students share the goals they defined with the whole class.

7a. Have each student think of a goal in her own life that she would like to define. One way to think of goals is to define <u>physical</u> goals (e.g., losing weight), <u>emotional</u> goals (e.g., responding to feeling with family) or <u>intellectual</u> goals (e.g., reading up on current events).

b. Have 2-3 students share their goals. Then ask students to define their goals using the six questions. Pair students in dyads to help one another complete this exercise.

8. Tell students that defining the goal prepares you to write a

successful plan for reaching the goal.

"IF YOU HELP YOUR LEARNERS DEFINE THEIR GOALS, YOU CAN HELP THEM PLAN TO REACH THEIR GOALS SO THEY CAN BE EFFECTIVE IN THEIR LEARNING."

Use the following summary form to help students summarize the skill of defining the goal. Students should use pages 157-162.

9. Possible Homework Assignment

Have students:

a. Write a brief summary of a group of fictional learners.

b. Write a feeling and meaning response to the learners.

c. Write 3 personalized responses.

d. Write a personalized understanding response.

e. Define the goal using the six questions.

10. Review with the students the steps they originally outlined to prepare for teaching a lesson in addition. Make sure they understand the important role played by attending, responding and personalizing skills (i.e., these help determine where learners are and where they want or need to be). In addition, make sure students understand which of their original steps involved some aspect of goal-definition.

11. Outline a personalized learner problem for your students. (For example, you might say "Billy is a boy who feels dumb because he can't read out loud as quickly and accurately as any of the other children in his class.") Have each of your students outline the steps she or he would take to define this problem in terms of a specific goal.

12. Review your students' goal-definitions and the steps they took to

develop these definitions.  Make
sure that each student has answered
the six questions.  Emphasize the
point that no learner will be able
to achieve a goal until that goal
has been defined in specific terms
which she or he can understand.

# DEFINING THE GOAL - SUMMARY

**What is it?**

(Asking basic questions to determine exactly where the learners are going.)

**What does it do?**

(Makes the goal precise - you know what it involves.)

1. Helps the learner understand where she is going.

2. Increases the learners' chance of getting there.

**Why do it?**

1. Determine who is involved.

2. What is to be done.

3. What actions are to be performed.

4. Where will the action take place.

5. Why is the learner moving toward this goal?

**How do you do it?**

(Prior to any concrete action.)

**When/Where do you do it?**

1. Have you answered all of the basic interrogatives?

2. Is the goal defined so that you could tell when the learner reaches the goal?

**How do you know if you've done it right?**

# CHAPTER 6: DEVELOPING STEPS
(Pages 163-171)

## OUTLINE OF SUGGESTED TEACHING CHRONOLOGY

1. Have students take pre-test.
2. Review interpersonal skills previously studied.
3. Preview skill of developing steps.
4. Demonstrate and show how to perform the skill.
5. Do small-group practices.
6. Role-play developing steps with a learner.
7. Give applications of the skill to the students' lives.
8. Summarize the critical components of the skill of developing steps.
9. Discuss pre-test.
10. Conduct post-test.
11. Provide feedback to reinforce learning and growth.

# DEVELOPING STEPS

1. Give students the problem of directing a learner from your room to the nearest drinking fountain. Have students write down their directions. Ask 2-3 students to read their directions while you try to follow the directions. Do only what the students tell you - do not fill in directives they have left out. (E.g., if the students tell you to turn right, do so; but do not automatically stop facing in the correct direction unless the student told you how far to turn right and when to stop.) You will probably find that no one wrote a detailed enough series of directions to ensure reaching the fountain.

2. Discuss with the students the information they needed in order to write good directions (e.g., where learner was starting from, where the fountain was, how much learner already knew) and the relationship of attending, responding and personalizing to this information.

3. Ask students to identify what was missing that made the directions to the fountain insufficient to get the learner to the goal.

4a. Your students need to know the following:

   Developing steps means identifying how the learner can reach the goal.

   By developing steps, you can help learners to act to reach their goals and solve many classroom problems.

b. Develop a list of the effective ingredients of developing steps. Be sure to include these (you may want to put them on the chalkboard).

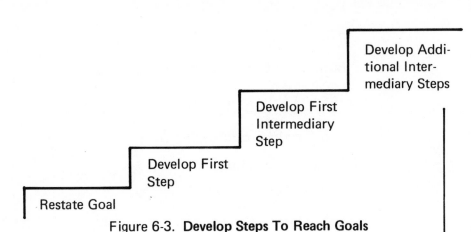

Develop Additional Intermediary Steps

Develop First Intermediary Step

Develop First Step

Restate Goal

Figure 6-3. **Develop Steps To Reach Goals**

c. Examine the steps developed on page 167 for Paul. Then look at the steps on page 170 for Paul. Note the first step, the first intermediary step and the additional intermediary step.

d. Tell your class that there are important things to ask in developing steps effectively:

1) "Is the first step so easy that the learner cannot fail?"

2) "Are all the steps put in measurable and observable terms so you can see or hear the learner do the step?"

3) "Do all the steps lead towards the defined goal?"

e. Ask students to use the 3 questions to check the steps for Paul on page 170.

5a. Have students develop steps for Mary on page 134. You might have students do this individually first and then develop steps as a large group. Write the steps the group develops on the chalkboard. (Save this program for further use in the next lesson.)

b. Divide class into small groups (2-4 members). Ask each group to define a learner goal and to develop a first step, a first intermediary step and additional intermediary steps to the goal.

Teachers cannot teach what they do not know. If a teacher cannot develop an effective program to reach the goal, the teacher and learner must find a person with the ability to write a program for that goal.

c.  Have each group share the programs they have developed with the whole class.  Students can suggest additional intermediary steps that would lead towards the goal.

Pair students in dyads.  Ask each pair to role-play a teacher/ learner interaction.  The "teacher" should attend, respond and personalize to help the "learner" explore and understand a problem. Then the "teacher" and "learner" should write the goal they define and develop steps to reach that goal.  They should check their work using the questions in 4d. Possible problem areas:

1)  Can't write an English paper.

2)  Unable to play basketball.

3)  Afraid to give a talk in class.

4)  Running for class president.

5)  Racial unrest.

6)  Sex discrimination.

7)  Deal with the physically handicapped.

b.  Have 1-2 dyads share the program they developed with the class, including the goal they defined and the steps developed.  Ask the class to check the work.

Students must understand that they should continue to respond to their learners as they develop programs. Learners' experiences are continually changing and the teacher must "stick with" the learners.  The reaction of the learner to the program is important!

7.  Have students list other uses for the skill of developing steps

by naming goals they now have or have had that they could reach by taking sequential steps.

8. Summarize developing steps with students.

"IF YOU DEVELOP STEPS WITH YOUR LEARNERS, THEY WILL BE ABLE TO MOVE FROM WHERE THEY ARE TO WHERE THEY NEED TO BE FOR EFFECTIVE LEARNING."

> Initiating is extremely important. Many discipline problems result from learners who have experienced only failures. Programs based on teacher attending, responding, personalizing and initiating help learners succeed. No one wants to fail, including learners. If students can help learners build successful programs, they will have fewer classroom problems.

Have students complete the following summary form.

9. Have students recall their earlier attempt to get a learner to the drinking fountain. How successful was it? What was lacking?

10a. Show students an audio-visual tape of a teacher/learner interaction that ends with the goal defined.

Ask students to develop steps for learner to take.

b. Have students exchange the programs they developed. Ask each student to check the first step, first intermediary step and additional intermediary steps. Is the first step easy? Are the steps observable and measurable? Do all steps lead towards the goal?

11. Reinforce students' growth by discussing benefits for them and for learners of developing measurable steps that lead to goals.

# DEVELOPING STEPS - SUMMARY

**What is it?** (Succession of measurable, observable, achievable behaviors.)

**What does it do?** (Moves the learner directly toward the goal.)

**Why do it?**
1. Takes learners from where they are to where they want or need to be.
2. Keeps learners "on track."
3. Ensures successful learning.

**How do you do it?**
1. Develop the first step.
2. Develop the first intermediary step.
3. Develop additional intermediary steps.

**When/Where do you do it?** (When learners want or need to reach a goal.)

**How do you know you've done it right?** (Ask: "Are there any gaps that the learner could fall through and not reach the goal?")

CHAPTER 6:  DEVELOPING SUB-STEPS

(Pages 171-175)

## OUTLINE OF SUGGESTED TEACHING CHRONOLOGY

1.  Have students take pre-test.

2.  Review previous initiating skills.

3.  Demonstrate and show how to perform the skill.

4.  Do large-group practices.

5.  Do small-group and individual practices.

6.  Give applications of the skill to the students' lives.

7.  Summarize the critical components of the skill of developing sub-steps.

8.  Assign homework.

9.  Discuss pre-test.

10. Conduct post-test.

11. Provide feedback to reinforce learning and growth.

## DEVELOPING SUB-STEPS

1.  Have students look at the programs on pages 170 and 173.  Ask them to identify which program would be more helpful to a learner who did not know how to study.

2a.  Discuss what is good about each program.  Why do the students feel one would be more useful than the other?

 b.  Discuss times with students when they have had a goal and several steps planned to reach the goal yet did not reach the goal.  What prevented them from reaching the goal?

FOR EXAMPLE:

Many students plan to enter a particular college yet are turned down; they may not have good enough grades, they may not meet a Language or Science requirement or they may simply have applied too late.  In general, the students failed to reach their goal because they did not plan enough details to ensure success.

3a.  Make sure students know that sub-steps are simply the details of the first and intermediary steps; they make sure there are no gaps.

 b.  Develop the components of developing sub-steps.  (You may want to put the diagram below on the board):

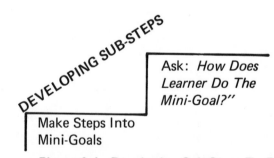

Figure 6-4. **Developing Sub-Steps To Reach Goals**

4.  Have students look at the programs on pages 173, 174 and 175.  They should notice that each step has

2-4 sub-steps listed underneath. As a group, have class add sub-steps to the program they developed for Mary (page 134) in the lesson on developing steps.

5a. Break class into small groups (3-4 members). Read aloud the information about Andy on page 139. Ask each group to define the goal and write a program which includes 4-6 steps with 2-3 sub-steps for each step.

b. Have 2 groups share the programs they developed with the whole class. Students can suggest additional steps and sub-steps.

c. Ask students to think of and define separate learner goals. They should then write a program with steps and sub-steps to reach the goals. Have students exchange completed programs for additional step and sub-step suggestions from other students.

d. Select 1-2 programs from 5c. Have 1-2 students role-play learners and use the program while the class watches. Rewrite the steps and sub-steps as necessary to make it possible for the "learners" to use the program. Tell students that an effective program is one that can be used to reach the goal.

6. Have each student think of another area of her life (non-teaching) where she could use a program to achieve a goal. Ask students to define these goals and write programs to reach the goals.

7a. Summarize developing sub-steps by having students complete the following summary form using pages 171-175. You might have the class compare answers to check their accuracy.

b. Tell students:

"IF YOU CAN DEVELOP SUB-STEPS FOR YOUR LEARNERS' PROGRAMS, YOU CAN HELP THEM GET TO WHERE THEY WANT AND NEED TO BE."

# DEVELOPING SUB-STEPS – SUMMARY

**What is it?**
(The specific and detailed behaviors which characterize achievement of the first and intermediary steps.)

**What does it do?**
(Details how to do the first and intermediary steps.)

**Why do it?**
(Makes the difference between learner failure and learner success.)

**How do you do it?**
(1. Make steps into mini-goals.
2. Ask: What must the learner do to reach this mini-goal?)

**When/Where do you do it**
(Before the learner begins to act.)

**How do you know if you've done it right?**
(If the learners achieve their goals.)

8.  Possible Homework Assignment:

    Have students define a learning
    goal of their own and write a
    program to reach that goal.  The
    program should include steps and
    sub-steps.  Students should also
    implement the program to check
    out if it is detailed enough to
    be effective.

9.  Discuss with students the pre-test
    from pages 154 and 155.  What was
    effective in their responses?
    What was lacking?

10. Have students complete the post-
    test on pages 181 and 182.

11. Use pages 183 and 184 to provide
    the students with feedback.
    Explore their increased ability
    to help solving learning problems.
    What effect does goal-acquisition
    have on difficult learners?

# CHAPTER 6: SUMMARY OF INITIATING

1. Review the major points of initiating. Be sure to include these points.

    Initiating skills allow you to provide your learners with constructive direction.

    Initiating helps your learners to act and achieve their goals.

    In order to effectively initiate, you must first be able to attend, respond and personalize with your learners.

    Initiating helps you to effectively control and solve classroom discipline problems.

2a. Select 3-4 students to role-play learners who are attempting to organize a class project such as a field trip but who keep breaking down and arguing. Ask 1 student to role-play the teacher. The "teacher" should attend, respond, personalize and initiate to demonstrate how things might be handled ideally.

b. When the "teacher" gets stuck or if things get off track, select another student to take over as "teacher." Continue this until the group has a program for organizing the project.

3. Critique the role-playing with your class. What was good? What could have been done differently? How could it have been done more effectively? What skills (attending, responding, personalizing, initiating) were strongest on the "teacher's" part? Which were weakest?

4. Divide class into 3 groups. Have one group list ways to use initiating at home, another list ways to use it at work and the third list ways to use it in the community. Ask the whole class to check to see if attending, responding and personalizing would also be useful in these situations.

5. Summarize the skills studied so far and the relationship between

the behaviors.  You may want to
put Figure 6-5 on the chalkboard
or an overhead projector.

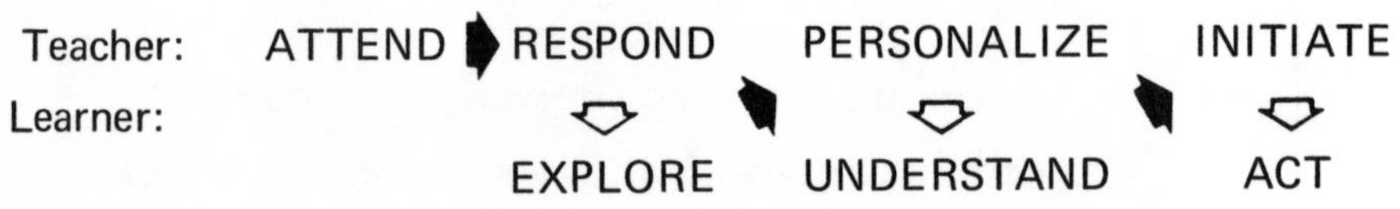

Teacher:  ATTEND ▶ RESPOND    PERSONALIZE    INITIATE
Learner:            ▽        ◥      ▽      ◥     ▽
          EXPLORE    UNDERSTAND    ACT

Figure 6-5. **Classroom interpersonal skills model**

"IF YOU CAN INITIATE WITH YOUR
LEARNERS, YOU CAN HELP THEM ACT
ON THEIR PROBLEMS AND ACHIEVE
THEIR LEARNING GOALS."

UNIT 7:  PREPARING YOUR LEARNERS FOR LEARNING

Concept:          Interpersonal <u>Skills</u>
                  <u>Scale</u> -a scale for
                  discriminating communica-
                  tion effectiveness

Principle:        <u>If</u> the teachers learn to
                  discriminate communica-
                  tion effectiveness, <u>then</u>
                  they will be able to
                  shape their effectiveness
                  <u>so</u> <u>that</u> they will facili-
                  tate their learners'
                  learning.

Skills            Learning to discriminate
Objective:;       effectiveness.

**OBJECTIVE**
**INTERPERSONAL COMMUNICATION**
**(p 192)**

5.0  Developing step-by-step program to achieve goals
4.5  Defining learners' goals
4.0  Personalizing learners' understanding of learning goals
3.5  Personalizing meaning of learners' expression
3.0  Responding interchangeably to feeling and meaning of learners' expressions
2.5  Responding to feeling of learners' expressions
2.0  Responding to content of learners' expressions
1.5  Expressions related to learners
1.0  Expressions unrelated to learners

**Skills Program:**   Levels

**Skills Feedback:**  Post-Test (pp 195-202)

# CHAPTER 7: PREPARING YOUR LEARNERS FOR LEARNING
## (Pages 186-206)

## OUTLINE OF SUGGESTED TEACHING CHRONOLOGY

1.  Review major points.

2.  Have small groups prepare review presentations.

3.  Conduct post-test.

4.  Provide student feedback and evaluation.

5.  Develop application programs.

6.  Assign homework.

7.  Summarize model.

PREPARING YOUR LEARNERS FOR LEARNING

1.  Have class recall the learning
    model including all skills.
    Write the model on the board as
    they identify the components.

**PHASES OF LEARNING**

| | | I | II | III |
|---|---|---|---|---|
| Teacher: | Helping Skills | Attending ▶ Responding | Personalizing | Initiating |
| Learner: | Learning Skills | Exploration | Understanding | Acting |

Figure 7-1. **Classroom interpersonal skills model**

"ALL TEACHING BEGINS WITH ATTEND-
ING TO YOUR LEARNERS AND ENDS
WITH INITIATING TO HELP THEM
ACT."

2a. Break class into 4 small groups.
    Ask each group to prepare a re-
    view of one of the major skill
    areas of attending, responding,
    personalizing and initiating.
    Each small group should include

the following things in their
review:

1)  <u>what</u> the skill is and <u>what</u>
    <u>it</u> <u>does</u>;

2)  <u>why</u> the skill is important;

3)  <u>how</u> to do the skill; and

4)  a <u>demonstration</u> of a
    teacher-learner(s) inter-
    action which focuses on
    using the skill effectively
    in the interaction.

Skills to be covered include:

5)  <u>attending</u> - attending physi-
    cally, observing, listening;

6)  <u>responding</u> - responding to
    feeling, responding to
    meaning;

7)  <u>personalizing</u> - laying a
    base, personalizing responses,
    personalizing understanding;
    and

8)  <u>initiating</u> - defining the
    goal, developing steps,
    developing sub-steps.

b. Have each group present its review to the class. Each student should make sure she understands the skill being reviewed.

3a. Review the rating scale presented on page 192 with your students.

b. Have students complete the post-test exercises on pages 196, 197 and 198.

4a. Have students complete their discrimination score using the chart on page 200.
Rate students' communication levels for the exercises on page 196. If students had a discrimination score of .5 or lower, they may rate their own responses.

Ask students to complete the chart on page 202. This will help them to compare their interpersonal communication level prior to the class to their present level.

Discuss implications of their growth in interpersonal skills.

For Example:

1) "What difference will it make for you as a teacher?"

2) "What difference will it make for your learners?"

3) "How will you be able to better achieve your teaching goals?"

4) "How will it impact your classroom?"

5. Have students develop individual programs for using the interpersonal skills they have studied. Students should identify teaching situations in which they are presently involved where they can use the skills. Tell students to define their goals and develop steps and sub-steps using the initiating skills they learned (pages 171 and 174 provide an example).

6. Suggested Homework Assignments:

a. Review The Skills of Teaching: Interpersonal Skills.

b.  Apply programs developed in step
5 above.  Rewrite program according to feedback from using program.

7.  Draw the learning model on the
board again.  Remind students
that interpersonal skills make a
difference in the classroom.

"IF YOU ATTEND, RESPOND, PERSONAL-
IZE AND INITIATE WITH YOUR LEARN-
ERS, YOU WILL BE ABLE TO CONTROL
YOUR CLASS AND HELP YOUR LEARNERS
LEARN WHAT THEY NEED TO KNOW."

# UNIT 8:  EXAMINATIONS AND GRADING

This unit contains both knowledge assessments (multiple-choice and short-answer essay items) and skill assessments (communication and discrimination items). The knowledge assessments are grouped by chapter so that they can be used as quizzes or combined into mid-term and final exams. The skill assessments are grouped into pre-and post- measures that can be used to measure student skill-gains over the duration of the course.

Additional sources for grading your students include:

a. class participation and attendance;

b. final ability to use inter-personal skills.

## Class participation and attendance.

Since a course based upon this text will involve a great many in-class practices and exercises, you may wish to include this area in your grading as students' performance in class will reflect, to a high degree, their ability to use the substance of the course in their own settings.

## Final ability to use interpersonal skills.

You may wish to compute this from any or all of 3 sources: (1) post-tests scores as each unit on individual skills is completed; (2) final demonstration by students of the skills during class; and (3) brief visits to students' work or application settings.

## CHAPTERS 1 AND 2: INTRODUCTION AND DEVELOPING YOUR LEARNING RELATIONSHIP

10 Questions

## MULTIPLE-CHOICE QUESTIONS

(asterisks * indicate best answers)

1. A basic ingredient of learning is motivating the learners to learn by:

   a. Controlling and disciplining your students.

   *b. Demonstrating that you can help them to learn.

   c. Asking exciting questions.

   d. Decorating your classroom in bright colors.

   Page 7

2. As a teacher, you will want to help your learners grow:

   *a. Physically, intellectually, emotionally and socially.

   b. Intellectually and socially.

   c. Intellectually, socially and emotionally.

   d. Intellectually and emotionally.

   Page 7

3. All teaching is done in the context of:

   a. A classroom.

   b. A skilled, professional teacher.

   *c. An interpersonal relationship.

   d. A structural, supervised learning exercise.

   Page 9

4. The first set of teaching skills are really:

   a. Planning skills.

   b. Curriculum development skills.

   *c. Interpersonal skills.

   d. Specialty area skills.

   Page 9

5. How the teacher deals with learners' interpersonal communications and expressions determines:

   *a. Whether she helps or harms a learner's learning efforts.

   b. Whether she gets pay raises or not.

   c. Whether she likes her learners or not.

d.    Whether she stays in teaching or not.

Page 17

6.    The two basic dimensions of interpersonal communication are:

a.    Attending, listening.

*b.   Responsive, initiative.

c.    Listening, responding.

d.    Attending, responding.

Page 22

## SHORT-ANSWER QUESTIONS (appropriate answers follow each question)

1.    What are the major skills the teacher uses in developing interpersonal relationships with her learners?

a.    Attends physically to her learners.

b.    Observes and listens to her learners.

c.    Responds to her learners.

d.    Understands her learners.

e.    Initiates with her learners.

Pages 12-16

2.    What does responsiveness mean?

The teacher's responsive statement shows she understands where the learner is and how the learner feels.  A statement that is high in responsiveness will contain a feeling word.

Page 22

3.    What does initiative mean?

Initiative means giving direction and guidance.  Initiative means helping the learners' understand where they want to be.  Sometimes this is in the form of advice or encouragement.

4.    Draw the learning model below. Include both helping and learning skills.

## CHAPTER 3:  ATTENDING SKILLS
### 30 Questions

## MULTIPLE-CHOICE QUESTIONS

1.    Attending skills include the behaviors of:

a.    Listening and responding.

b.    Responding, personalizing and initiating.

*c. Attending physically, observing and listening.

d. Squaring, recalling content and communicating.

Page 55

2. Ratings of level 3.0 or above for attending indicate that the teacher is:

*a. Looking at the learners while squaring with them.

b. Looking at the learners no matter how the teacher's body is positioned.

c. Getting the class to quiet down.

d. Watching the class to keep the learners quiet.

Page 54

3. Attending skills set the stage for responding by:

a. Giving learners the signal that the teacher is ready to begin.

b. Giving the teacher the cues she needs to develop good responses.

c. Giving the teacher the chance to reinforce her learners.

d. All of the above.

*e. a and b.

Page 55

4. The four dimensions of attending physically are:

*a. Contextual, presentational, postural and visual.

b. Eye contact, squaring, leaning and no distractions.

c. Eye contact, observing, listening and responding.

d. Caring, interest, concern and warmth.

Page 55

5. When considering how the teacher appears to the learner, what is most important?

a. Age, race and sex.

b. Age.

*c. Behavior and appearance.

d. Attitudes.

Page 57

118

6. It is important for the teacher not to tilt her head while attending physically because she wants to communicate:

   a. Balance.

*b. Strength.

   c. Calmness.

   d. Good posture.

Page 61

7. Which, if any, of the following statements are not true?

   a. Teachers should circulate while talking to a group.

*b. It is all right to only half-turn if the teacher is writing on the board; she does not need to square with the learners.

   c. The teacher should place herself so that she can see all of her learners.

*d. Leaning or sitting on the teacher's desk will help her to focus her attention.

Pages 63-64

8. One of the most important behaviors for making contact with learners as individuals is:

   a. Touching them.

   b. Smiling.

*c. Making eye contact.

   d. Saying good morning.

Page 59

9. Appearance cues might include:

   a. The organization of the learner's desk.

*b. The age, clothes, body build, race, sex of the learner.

   c. The mannerisms and habits of the learner.

   d. The home life of the learner.

Page 67

10. Energy level has a direct relationship to the learner's ability to:

   a. Be happy.

   b. Get along well.

   c. Be likable.

*d. Learn.

Page 68

11. Learner's eye contact can tell the teacher a great deal about the _____ of the learner's commitment to conquer the learning.

   a.  Effectiveness.
   *b.  Intensity.
   c.  Sureness.
   d.  Implication.

   Page 70

12. Recalling the learner's expression verbatim will help teachers to:

   *a.  Formulate an accurate response to the learner.
   b.  Attend closely to the learner.
   c.  Observe the learner accurately.
   d.  React quickly.

   Page 76

13. One way for a teacher to check out the accuracy of her listening in the classroom is to:

   a.  Ask the learner to repeat what the learner said.
   b.  Respond to the learner's statement.
   c.  Wait for the learner to say it again.
   *d.  Repeat the gist of what the learner said.

   Page 77

14. Attending to learners will communicate:

   a.  The teacher's desire to move the lesson on.
   b.  The teacher's concern with how she looks.
   *c.  The teacher's interest in and concern with the learners.
   d.  The teacher's confidence in herself.

   Page 78

15. Mastery of attending behaviors insures that:

   *a.  Effective teaching will be possible.
   b.  All learners will like the teacher.
   c.  The teacher will be promoted.
   d.  The teacher will like all learners.

   Page 85

## SHORT-ANSWER QUESTIONS

1. How do attending skills set the stage for responding to learners?

   a. Gives learners the signal that the teacher is ready to pay full attention to them.

   b. Gives the teacher the needed cues for delivering good responses to the learners.

   Page 55

2. What issues might a teacher consider when preparing the environment to attend to learners?

   a. Attractiveness

   -Can the learner find something of himself or herself in the classroom?

   Functionality

   -Are seats spaced so the teacher can attend to each learner individually?

   -Are visual materials relevant rather than distracting?

   Page 56

3. How should a teacher dress for teaching?

   Appropriately for the role as a teacher who has something to offer - not like one of the learners.

   Page 57

4. What benefits does the teacher receive from attending to her learners?

   a. Attending to learners increases their attending to the teacher.

   b. The teacher will be ready to respond to and teach effectively if she knows her learners as individuals.

   Page 49

5. What are the behaviors of attending physically in the classroom?

   a. Squaring.

   b. Leaning.

   c. Eye contact.

   d. Closing the distance between teacher and learner.

e.    Eliminating distractions.

Ch. 3

6.    What behavior(s) does the teacher
      need before she can observe
      learners?

      Attending physically.

      Page 55

7.    Name some of the important cues
      the teacher should observe learn-
      ers for:

      a.    Context and environment.
      b.    Appearance.
      c.    Behavior.
      d.    Posture.
      e.    Eye contact.

      Pages 66-70

8.    One of the most important groups
      of behaviors to observe are those
      that indicate _____.

      Energy Level.

      Page 68

9.    The posture of learners can tell
      the teacher many things about the
      learners.  What are some of
      these?

a.    Their level of attentiveness.  121
b.    Their past learning history.
c.    Their interest and investment
      in learning.
d.    Their past experiences with
      either people or material.
e.    Their current experience and
      relationship with you.

      Page 69

10.   What are the steps of observing
      learners?

      a.    Observe context and environment.
      b.    Observe appearance.
      c.    Observe behavior.
      d.    Draw inferences.

      Ch 3

11.   Why is it important to observe
      learners?

      a.    It is a rich source of cues
            for responding to them.
      b.    It helps the teacher to see
            them as individuals.

      Page 65

12.   What behavior(s) facilitate
      listening behavior?

      a.    Attending physically.

b. Observing.

Page 75

13. What is meant by listening?

Hearing what the learners have said.

Page 75

14. Why is it important to suspend judgment when listening to learners?

You will not hear what they actually say if you get caught up in your own reaction.

Page 75

15. What things specially related to learners' learning can the teacher learn by listening to them?

a. Whether they are ready to get involved in the learning or not.

b. What materials they need to complete the task.

c. How they are feeling about themselves in relation to the task.

Page 78

# CHAPTER 4: RESPONDING SKILLS

20 Questions

## MULTIPLE-CHOICE QUESTIONS

1. Responding means:

   a. Telling the learner what the teacher thinks.

   b. Answering and asking quesions.

   *c. Communicating an understanding of the learner's experience.

   d. Giving the learner direction or advice.

   Page 87

2. A minimally effective response (level 3.0) will enable the learner to:

   *a. Explore himself.

   b. Get his way.

   c. Solve the problem.

   d. Understand himself.

   Page 92

3. A high responsive/low initiative response:

*a. Captures the learner's feeling and reason for the feeling.

b. Captures where the learner wants to go.

c. Summarizes the content of what the learner said.

d. Asks a meaningful question.

Page 92

4. If the teacher responds to the learner, it is <u>not</u> true that _____.

a. She will gain the necessary understanding for providing direction and guidance.

b. The learners will be more open to guidance and direction.

*c. She will have effectively taught the learners what they need to know.

d. The learners will be certain the teacher understands where they are.

Page 92

5. If the teacher responds to the learner's feeling, then _____.

a. The learner will know the teacher thinks that is the right way to feel about the situation.

*b. The learner will know the teacher understands her feeling.

c. The learner will know the teacher likes her.

d. The teacher will be ready to tell the learner what to do.

Page 96

6. Feelings can be grouped by _____ and _____.

a. Thinking and debating.

b. Age and sex.

c. Good and bad.

*d. Categories and intensity.

Page 98

7. In order to respond to feeling effectively, the teacher must be able to identify a feeling word that is_____ the learner's original expression.

a.   Close to.

b.   Better than.

*c.   Interchangeable with.

d.   Different from.

Page 106

8.   Select the minimum number of learners a teacher should respond to each day.

a.   5-15.

b.   20-40.

c.   1-5.

*d.   15-20.

Page 117

9.   How many learners can a teacher communicate understanding to at one time?

a.   one.

b.   two.

c.   three.

*d.   an entire group.

Page 118

10.   Mastery of responding skills will help the teacher to _____.

a.   Be ready to solve discipline problems.

b.   Facilitate the learner's exploration of themselves.

c.   Diagnose the learner's learning problems.

d.   Control the class.

*e.   All of the above.

Page 124.

## SHORT-ANSWER QUESTIONS

1.   Why is responding in the classroom important?

a.   It facilitates the learner's exploration of where they are in relation to themselves, the learning material and their world.

b.   It lays a base for personalizing the learner's understanding.

c.   It facilitates working together to solve problems and going on to achieve learning goals.

Page 87-88

2.   What behaviors make it possible for the teacher to respond accurately to her learners?

a. Attending physically.

b. Observing.

c. Listening.

Page 92

3. What is a feeling word?

It is a word referring directly to a feeling, i.e.,
"mad."

Page 93

4. What is the goal of the first
stage of human relations?

To understand what the
learner is saying and how
she feels about it (i.e., to
respond).

Page 93

5. What are the steps of responding
to feeling?

a. Attend - attend physically,
observe, listen.

b. Repeat verbatim.

c. Ask: "How does that make me
(as the learner) feel?"

d. Select one feeling word.

e. Respond "You feel _____."

Pages 93-97

6. What are the feeling categories
given in Skills of Teaching:
Interpersonal Skills?

a. Happy.

b. Sad.

c. Angry.

d. Confused.

e. Scared.

f. Weak.

g. Strong.

Page 99

7. What are the intensities by which
feeling words can be grouped?

a. Strong.

b. Mild.

c. Weak.

Page 100

8. What are the sub-steps for selecting a feeling word?

a. Select a feeling category.

b. Review words in that category.

c. Decide on the intensity of
the feeling.

d.  Recall a word of the appro-
    priate intensity in that
    category.

e.  Make sure it is a useful
    feeling word.

                        Page 100

9.  What is responding to meaning?

    Communicating understanding
    of the reason for the feel-
    ing.

                        Page 114

10. Why is it important to respond to
    learners' feelings and meaning?

    a.  Such responses facilitate
        learner exploration of where
        they are.

    b.  Without this minimally
        effective response, there
        can be no effective teaching.

                        Page 116

# CHAPTER 5:  PERSONALIZING SKILLS

## 25 Questions

## MULTIPLE-CHOICE QUESTIONS

1.  Personalizing means:

    a.  Talking directly to an indivi-
        dual.

    b.  Sharing the teacher's experi-
        ence with learners.

    *c. Using the teacher's experience
        to help the learner determine
        where they are in relation to
        where they want to go.

    d.  Visiting the learner at home
        to learn about his family and
        background.

                        Page 126

2.  What is the source of the teacher's
    understanding?

    *a. The learner's deficit behavior.

    b.  Objective tests such as I.Q.

    c.  Discussions with other teach-
        ing staff.

    d.  Asking the learner to tell you
        specific things.

                        Page 127

3. What is the key to personalizing?

   a. Inclusion of a specific learner problem which is causing her present feelings.

   b. Providing a number of steps for achievement of a goal.

   c. Reflecting on where the learner wants to be.

   d. All of the above.

   e. A and B.

   f. B and C.

   *g. A and C.

   Page 129

4. Another term for personalizing is:

   a. Communicating.

   *b. Additive understanding responses.

   c. Experiential responses.

   d. Teacher self-disclosure.

   Page 130

5. Laying an interchangeable base with the learners means:

   a. Working with them at least 1/2 hour.

   b. Repeating the statements they have made.

   *c. Responding to the learners' feelings and meaning at least six times.

   d. Teaching the learners to respond.

   Page 131

6. By personalizing responses to learners and involving them directly in their expression of their experience, the teacher:

   a. Identifies who is to blame or at fault for the problem.

   *b. Helps the learner to take responsibility for himself.

   c. Encourages the learner to feel like a victim.

   d. Frees herself of any responsibility for the learner's problems.

   Page 135

7. Which response form below reflects a personalized problem response?

   a. "You feel___ because____."

   b. "You feel___because you ____."

*c.    "You feel____because you can't____."

d.     "Your goal is ____."

Page 137

9. The learner's behavior deficit is a deficit in her:

*a.    Repertoire of responses.

b.     Home life.

c.     Relationship with fellow students.

d.     Relationship with her teachers.

Page 137

10. At a minimum, how many personalized responses in a row must the teacher be able to make before moving on to additive responses?

a.     Three.

*b.    Six.

c.     Twelve.

d.     Twenty.

Page 139

11. The emphasis of responses which personalize understanding is:

a.     The feeling.

*b.    The meaning.

c.     Initiative.

d.     Timing.

Page 141

12. Personalizing yields responses which are:

a.     High responsive - low initiative.

b.     Low responsive - low initiative.

*c.    High responsive - high initiative.

d.     Low responsive - high initiative.

Page 143

13. Identify the statement(s) below which are true.

*a.    If you have a responsive base, you may choose to confront a learner in order to facilitate understanding.

*b.    Confrontations may involve a discrepancy between where learners are and where you believe they need to be.

*c.    Confrontation is never necessary and never sufficient.

d. Confrontation is a preferred response for teachers to effectively deal with learn- ers.

Page 146

14. A rating of level 4.0 would be a response which:

a. Responds to content.

b. Responds to feeling and meaning.

c. Personalizes the feeling and meaning

*d. Personalizes understanding.

Page 150

15. Mastery of personalizing will:

*a. Take the teacher a step closer to effective teaching.

b. Make the teacher an effec- tive teacher.

c. Allow the teacher to manipu- late the learners.

d. Focus the teacher on good relationships and not on teaching.

Page 151

1. Why is it important to personalize the teacher's responses to her learners?

a. Promotes deeper understanding of the learners.

b. Helps the learner to take control of her life and her problems.

c. Facilitates the learner's understanding of where she is and where she wants to be.

d. Prepares for development of goals and effective action programs.

Page 126

2. Why is it important to have laid an interchangeable base with the learners before personalizing?

An interchangeable base pre- pares the teacher and the learners to understand at a level the learners do not express explicitly.

Page 127

3.  Why is personalizing important as a preliminary step for initiating?

    Understanding where the learner wants to be:

    a.  Helps to establish the goal of the program.
    b.  Helps to establish the first step of the program.

    Page 130

4.  What are the steps of personalizing?

    Ch. 5

    Personalize
    Understanding
    1) Personalize the goal

    Personalize
    the responses
    1) Personalize the Meaning
    2) Personalize the problem
    3) Personalize the feeling

    Lay an interchangeable base

5.  What question can the teacher ask herself in order to personalize the meaning of her response?

    "What are the implications of the experience for the learner's behavior of life,"

    Page 136

6.  What criteria are useful in determining when the teacher might move from laying an interchangeable base to personalizing responses?

    a.  What kind of relationship the teacher has with the learners.
    b.  The level of exploration the learners are engaging in.

    Page 138

7.  How can the teacher determine if her responses have been interchangeable?

    The learner will continue to explore new material.

8.  What is the goal of personalizing understanding by personalizing the goal?

Establish a direction which the learners can use within their frames of reference.

Page 140

9. The personalized goal is simply the _____ of the personalized problem.

"Flip-side"

Page 140

10. Personalizing skills prepare your learners for learning because _____.

They will trust you because you can understand them and help them to understand themselves.

Page 151

## CHAPTER 6: INITIATING SKILLS

### 17 Questions

## MULTIPLE-CHOICE QUESTIONS

1. The highest level of initiative skills involves:

a. Observing.

b. Responding to feeling.

c. Personalizing the goals.

*d. Program Development.

Page 153

2. The source of the teacher's ability to develop programs is her:

a. Understanding of where the learners are.

b. Understanding of where the learners want to be.

c. Understanding of where she is in the lesson.

*d. All of the above.

Page 154

3. A response which was rated level 5.0 would communicate:

a. How the learner could reach her goal.

b. Where the learner is.

c. Where the learner needs or what to be.

*d. All of the above.

Page 156

4. The 3 major steps in initiating skills are:

a.   Defining the goal, assessing self and developing steps.

*b.   Defining the goal, developing steps, developing sub-steps.

c.   Defining where at, defining goal, developing sub-steps.

d.   Attend, respond, personalize.

Ch. 6

5.   The first step of a program should:

a.   Be so simple the learner can easily take it.

b.   Move the learner in a direct line toward the goal.

c.   Be defined in measurable, observable and doable terms.

*d.   All of the above.

Page 163

6.   The first intermediary step should be:

a.   Close to the goal.

b.   Close to the first step.

*c.   Approximately halfway between the first step and the goal.

d.   It makes no difference.

7.   The number of additional intermediate steps needed in a program is:

a.   3 or 4.

b.   5 to 9.

c.   10 to 15.

*d.   Variable; there should be enough to eliminate "gaps" in the program.

Page 169

8.   When developing sub-steps, each step becomes:

a.   Unnecessary.

*b.   A mini-goal.

c.   A sub-step.

d.   A deadline.

Page 172

9.   The more detail, the higher the probability of the learners:

a.   Failure to achieve the program's goals.

b.   Seeking a less complusive teacher to receive help from.

c. Success in achieving the program's goals.

d. Being overwhelmed by the task.

Page 177

10. The teacher's effectiveness in initiating is totally dependent upon her effectiveness in:

a. Attending, responding.

b. Exploration, understanding, action.

c. Attending, responding, action.

*d. Attending, responding, personalizing.

Page 185

## SHORT-ANSWER QUESTIONS

1. Why are initiative skills important in the classroom?

a. Without them, there is no culmination to the helping process.

b. They lay the base for the teaching process.

c. They facilitate the learner's ability to act.

Page 153

2. What are the six questions which are used to define the goals.

a. Who is involved?

b. What is to be done?

c. When are the actions to be performed?

d. Where will the action take place.

e. How can the action be performed?

f. Why is the learner moving toward this goal?

Page 157

3. What is the purpose of asking and answering the six basic questions in defining the goal?

a. To make sure that each learner's goal is defined in observable, measurable, useful and achieveable terms.

b. To ensure that each learners' growth is as tangible and real as possible.

Page 157

4. What are the behaviors that lead to developing steps?

a. Establish the first step.

b. Establish the first intermediary step.

c. Establish additional intermediary steps.

Page 163-167

5. Why is it important for steps to
be defined in observable, measurable,
functional and achieveable terms?

It is the only way for a
learner to know when he or
she has taken the step and
where he or she now is in
relation to the goal.

6. What question does the teacher
ask herself in providing sub-
steps for a learner?

"What must the learner do
specifically in order to
complete this step?"

Page 172

7. What should an effective teacher
do if the learner's goal requires
special expertise that the learner does not have?

Develop a program for herself or the learner to find
out the information necessary to develop a program in
the area requiring special
expertise.

Page 177

# CHAPTER 7: PREPARING YOUR LEARNERS FOR LEARNING

5 Questions

## MULTIPLE-CHOICE QUESTIONS

1. It is important that interpersonal
skills are used to:

*a. Individualize your treatment
of the different learners.

b. Standardize your treatment
of different learners.

c. Organize your treatment of
different learners.

d. Operationalize your treatment of different learners.

Page 190

2. Teaching is:

a. An "edge" system.

*b.    The preferred mode of helping anyone to get anywhere.

c.    Based only on the teacher's frame of reference.

d.    Primarily program development.

Page 206

## SHORT-ANSWER QUESTIONS

1. How might the phases of learning be emphasized differently with different levels of learners?

    a.    It is important to emphasize exploration with low-level functioning learners.

    b.    With higher-level functioning learners, you may move quickly through exploration to stress understanding and action.

Page 190

2. What 3 questions are important to consider when the teacher is planning educational activities?

    a.    Do these activities respond to where the learners are?

    b.    Do they express an understanding of where the learners want to be in relation to where they are?

    c.    Do they initiate programs for how to get the learners from where they are to where they want to be?

Page 191

3. What is the scale for rating responses: What does each level mean:

Level 1.0 - no expression or expression unrelated to learners.

Level 1.5 - expression related to learners - usually poor guidance.

Level 2.0 - responding to content - usually some guidance for learners.

Level 2.5 - responding to feeling of learners.

Level 3.0 - responding interchange-
          ably to feeling and
          meaning of learners.

Level 3.5 - personalizing the mean-
          ing of learners.

Level 4.0 - personalizing under-
          standing of learner's
          goals.

Level 4.5 - defining the goal in
          terms of steps to
          learner's goal.

Level 5.0 - developing a step-by-
          step program to
          achieve learner's
          goal.

# SKILL ASSESSMENTS: COMMUNICATION AND DISCRIMINATION ITEMS

This section contains 16 learner stimulus expressions and 5 teacher responses to each stimulus with ratings for each teacher response.

You can create a test of your students' communication skills by listing just the learner expressions and asking your students to write responses to each of them. A test of your students' ability to discriminate helpful responses can be created by listing the stimulus expressions and alternate responses exactly as shown and asking your students to rate each response using the scale on page 19 of The Skills of Teaching: Interpersonal Skills.

Here are standard instructions you can use with each test.

Instructions to be read for communication test:

"The following excerpts involve a number of expressions of problems made by students. Please formulate the most helpful or most effective responses which you might make to each of these expressions. Be as helpful as you can in communicating your understanding and any helpful, new direction for the student. Formulate your response just as you would if you were talking directly with the student.

In formulating your responses, assume that you have been interacting with the students for some time before they present you with the problems."

Instructions to be read for discrimination test:

"The following excerpts involve a number of responses that a teacher might make to problems presented by students. Following each expression there are five alternate teacher responses. Rate these responses from 1 to 5 as follows:

1.0- Very ineffective - No understanding or direction.

2.0- Ineffective - No understanding, some direction

3.0- Minimally Effective - Understanding, no direction.

138

4.0- Effective - understanding and direction.

5.0- Very effective - Understanding and specific direction.

Assume that they have been interacting with the teachers for some time before presenting the teacher with the following problems."

## Student Expressions and Teacher Responses

EXCERPT I

"Sometimes she acts like she's my best friend, and the next day she acts like she doesn't even know me."

HELPER RESPONSES TO EXCERPT I

1.   "You'll just have to go and ask her what's going on."

2.   "You feel confused because you just don't know where you stand with her and you'd like to."

3.   "You feel upset because she changes so much."

4.   "Girls act that way at this age."

5.   "It really hurts a lot because you like her so much and yet you get to feel funny about yourself. Let's see if we can find a way to make it so you don't feel so funny about yourself anymore."

EXCERPT II

"I do my homework every night, but as hard as I try I can't get that stupid stuff.."

HELPER RESPONSES TO EXCERPT II

1.   "You feel angry because you can't handle that stuff and you really want to."

2.   "It makes you angry with yourself because you get to wondering if you're good enough.  Let's sit down and develop a little program for handling your homework."

3.   "Don't give up because you have what it takes."

4.   "You feel angry because that stuff is so hard."

5.   "It'll work out - it always does."

EXCERPT III

"D..d..don't tell my father - please don't tell my father!"

HELPER RESPONSES TO EXCERPT III

1. "Why, what do you think he'll do?"

2. "I think you're just going to have to go home and work it out with him."

3. "You're scared because you can't defend what you've done.  Let's see if we can't do something so this doesn't happen again in the future."

4. "You're frightened because he may punish you."

5. "You're scared because you don't know what he'll do."

EXCERPT IV

"I don't want to leave this school and all my friends, but Mom says we got to move because of Dad's job."

HELPER RESPONSES TO EXCERPT IV

1. "You feel down because you're not sure you can make it in the new place and you'd like to."

2. "You feel bad because everyone who matters will be left behind."

3. "I had to move when I was a kid, but I found I was able to make new friends by really working hard at it."

4. "You're sad because you're not sure you can make new friends.  Let's sit down and work out a little program for making friends in your new home."

5. "What kind of work does your father do?"

EXCERPT V

"You never give me a chance - you always pick someone else - you don't care about me - you're not my friend anymore."

HELPER RESPONSES TO EXCERPT V

1. "You're furious with me because you don't know where I'm coming from. Let me see if I can help you with that."

2. "All you have to do is work harder, and I'll be your friend again."

3. "What makes you feel that way?"

4. "You're really upset because you don't know where you stand with me and you'd like to."

5. "You're really angry with me because I let you down."

EXCERPT VI

"They're always picking on me - you know, ganging up on me and pushing me around - I don't even want to go to school anymore."

HELPER RESPONSES TO EXCERPT VI

1. "You're frightened because you really don't know what you're going to do."

2. "I wonder why they pick on you that way?"

3. "Just stay away from them and come to me if they give you any trouble."

4. "You feel scared because they try to hurt you."

5. "You're scared because you don't know why they're so mean to you. Let's take a closer look at the situation where they pick on you."

EXCERPT VII

"I never know if what I do is good or bad - you never tell me - how can I do the right thing?"

HELPER RESPONSES TO EXCERPT VII

1. "You're angry with me because you're not sure where you stand and you'd like to know."

2. "You're really upset because you don't think I care about you. Well I do, and from now on I'm going to make sure you know it."

3. "You feel confused because I haven't let you know where you stand."

4. "Well, how do you think you're doing?"

5. "Just listen to me carefully next time when I give directions and I'll repeat the instructions if you have problems."

EXCERPT VIII

"Joey's my best friend - it's really fun to go to school now."

HELPER RESPONSES TO EXCERPT VIII

1.  "You're really excited because you can have a lot of fun with Joey and that's the way you like things to be."

2.  "You'll have to work hard to keep a good friend."

3.  "Watch out for Joey - he gets into a lot of trouble."

4.  "It's really fun to be with Joey."

5.  "Hey, it's fun to be with you, too, when you're happy.  Let's just take some steps to make sure it stays this way."

EXCERPT IX

"I didn't think I could do it, but now I'm doing the best in the whole class.  I know I can make it."

HELPER RESPONSES TO EXCERPT IX

1.  "Keep up the good work."

2.  "You feel excited because you can handle that stuff.  Let's just plan some steps so that you can continue to handle it."

3.  "Now that you know that you have what it takes, you can start working even harder."

4.  "You feel pretty happy about everything."

5.  "You're really excited because you've got what it takes and that's the way you like it."

EXCERPT X

"I'm gonna get him back - no matter what you do - I'm gonna get him back!"

HELPERS RESPONSES TO EXCERPT X

1.  "You're furious because you haven't been able to handle him.  Let's sit down and see if we can find a way to make this turn out right."

2.  "You really ought to see if you can talk it over with him first before you do something stupid."

3. "You're so mad because you won't feel O.K. until you do get him."

4. "Are you fighting again?'

5. "You're really angry with him."

EXCERPT XI

"I'm going to miss you - can I come to visit you next year?"

HELPER RESPONSES TO EXCERPT XI

1. "Sure. I'll look forward to seeing you again. Be sure and look me up."

2. "We'll cross that bridge when we get to it."

3. "You're sad because you can't be sure that you'll feel that way about another teacher. I think we can take a few steps to make sure that you can."

4. "You feel sad about leaving."

5. "You feel bad because you're not sure you can feel this way about another teacher and you really want to."

EXCERPT XII

"Sometimes I think I'm dumb."

HELPER RESPONSES TO EXCERPT XII

1. "You feel sad because you don't seem to be who you want to be."

2. "Stop feeling sorry for yourself - and get to work - we both know you can do it."

3. "You feel bad about your work."

4. "You feel sad because you can't do the things you'd like to. I think there are a few simple steps you can take to make things better."

5. "We all feel that way some of the time."

EXCERPT XIII

"Miss Norman, I like you!"

HELPER RESPONSES TO EXCERPT XIII

1. "Most kiddies like their teachers."

2. "You're feeling pretty happy with me."

3. "Thank you, but now let's get that work done."

4.   "You really like me because you know I like you and that makes you feel good."

5.   "I love you, too.  Now let's make some plans so that we can do the things we need to do to keep it that way."

EXCERPT XIV

"Sometimes I like to go to school and sometimes I don't.  Sometimes I like my teacher and sometimes I don't."

HELPER RESPONSES TO EXCERPT XIV

1.   "What makes you feel that way?"

2.   "We're just going to have to work some more on that mixed-up feeling of yours."

3.   "It's pretty confusing to be up one minute and down the next. Maybe we can figure out why."

4.   "You feel confused because you can't feel up all the time and you'd like to."

5.   "You're really not sure where you stand."

EXCERPT XV

"I'm really worried.  If I don't make the last marking period, my Dad's sure gonna get me good."

HELPER RESPONSES TO EXCERPT XV

1.   "Well, we're going to have to get ourselves together before we face him."

2.   "You feel upset because he's really going to be angry."

3.   "I doubt your Dad will do anything."

4.   "You feel scared because you can't do anything about it and you'd like to."

5.   "You're frightened because you're always doing something to bring it on yourself.  Now if you don't want that to happen anymore, we're going to have to work out a little program."

EXCERPT XVI

(Child resting head on desk without talking.)

HELPER RESPONSES TO EXCERPT XVI

1.  "You're really tired but we'll have to work out some way to get you going again."

2.  "All right, everybody on their feet and stretch."

3.  "No sleeping in my class."

4.  "You're pretty tired but you'd like to get going."

5.  "You're pretty tired because that stuff just can't keep you awake."

Tables 8-1 and 8-2 on the following pages include the design for the alternate responses and the expert ratings for these responses. The design for the alternate responses includes varying the level of responsiveness and the level of initiative behavior. These dimensions are systematically varied at high (H) and low (L) levels in the following combinations.

1.0 LL -

This response is low on responding to where the student is and low on initiating in terms of where the student wants to be.

2.0 LH -

This response is low on responding to where the student is and moderately high on initiating in terms of giving advice about where the student wants to be.

3.0 HL -

This response is high on responding to the feeling and meaning of where the student is and low on initiating in terms of where the student wants to be.

4.0 HH -

This response is high on responding to the feeling and meaning of where the student is and high on initiating by personalizing the understanding of where the student wants to be.

5.0 HH+ -

This response is high on responding to the feeling and

meaning of where the student
is and high on initiating by
personalizing the understanding and developing first steps
for where the student wants to
be.

The alternate responses are randomly
ordered.  The trained rater's ratings
are the composite ratings of professionals who had demonstrated the validity
of their ratings in previous studies of
the effects of teaching relationships.

TABLE 8-1

Key to Design and Trained Rater's
Ratings of Teacher Responses to
Student Stimulus Expressions

| Student Stimulus Expression (Excerpts) | Teacher Responses | DESIGN | | Overall Ratings |
| --- | --- | --- | --- | --- |
| | | Level Of Responsiveness | Level Of Initiative | |
| I | 1 | L | H | 2.0 |
| | 2 | H | H | 4.0 |
| | 3 | H | L | 3.0 |
| | 4 | L | L | 1.0 |
| | 5 | H | H+ | 5.0 |
| II | 1 | H | H | 4.0 |
| | 2 | H | H+ | 5.0 |
| | 3 | L | H | 2.0 |
| | 4 | H | L | 3.0 |
| | 5 | L | L | 1.0 |
| III | 1 | L | L | 1.0 |
| | 2 | L | H | 2.0 |
| | 3 | H | H+ | 5.0 |
| | 4 | H | L | 3.0 |
| | 5 | H | H | 4.0 |
| IV | 1 | H | H | 4.0 |
| | 2 | H | L | 3.0 |
| | 3 | L | H | 2.0 |
| | 4 | H | H | 5.0 |
| | 5 | L | L | 1.0 |
| V | 1 | H | H+ | 5.0 |
| | 2 | L | H | 2.0 |
| | 3 | L | L | 1.0 |
| | 4 | H | H | 4.0 |
| | 5 | H | L | 3.0 |
| VI | 1 | H | H | 4.0 |
| | 2 | L | L | 1.0 |
| | 3 | L | H | 2.0 |
| | 4 | H | L | 3.0 |
| | 5 | H | H+ | 5.0 |
| VII | 1 | H | H | 4.0 |
| | 2 | H | H+ | 5.0 |
| | 3 | H | L | 3.0 |
| | 4 | L | L | 1.0 |
| | 5 | L | H | 2.0 |
| VIII | 1 | H | H | 4.0 |
| | 2 | L | H | 2.0 |
| | 3 | L | L | 1.0 |
| | 4 | H | L | 3.0 |
| | 5 | H | H+ | 5.0 |

TABLE 8-2
Key to Design and Trained Rater's
Ratings of Teacher Responses to
Student Stimulus Expressions

| Student Stimulus Expression (Excerpts) | Teacher Responses | DESIGN | | Overall Ratings |
|---|---|---|---|---|
| | | Level Of Responsiveness | Level Of Initiative | |
| IX | 1 | L | L | 1.0 |
| | 2 | H | H+ | 5.0 |
| | 3 | L | H | 2.0 |
| | 4 | H | L | 3.0 |
| | 5 | H | H | 4.0 |
| X | 1 | H | H+ | 5.0 |
| | 2 | L | H | 2.0 |
| | 3 | H | H | 4.0 |
| | 4 | L | L | 1.0 |
| | 5 | H | L | 3.0 |
| XI | 1 | L | H | 2.0 |
| | 2 | L | L | 1.0 |
| | 3 | H | H+ | 5.0 |
| | 4 | H | L | 3.0 |
| | 5 | H | H | 4.0 |
| XII | 1 | H | H | 4.0 |
| | 2 | L | H | 2.0 |
| | 3 | H | L | 3.0 |
| | 4 | H | H+ | 5.0 |
| | 5 | L | L | 1.0 |
| XIII | 1 | L | L | 1.0 |
| | 2 | H | L | 3.0 |
| | 3 | L | H | 2.0 |
| | 4 | H | H | 4.0 |
| | 5 | H | H+ | 5.0 |
| XIV | 1 | L | L | 1.0 |
| | 2 | L | H | 2.0 |
| | 3 | H | H+ | 5.0 |
| | 4 | H | H | 4.0 |
| | 5 | H | L | 3.0 |
| XV | 1 | L | H | 2.0 |
| | 2 | H | L | 3.0 |
| | 3 | L | L | 1.0 |
| | 4 | H | H | 4.0 |
| | 5 | H | H+ | 5.0 |
| XVI | 1 | H | H+ | 5.0 |
| | 2 | L | H | 2.0 |
| | 3 | L | L | 1.0 |
| | 4 | H | H | 4.0 |
| | 5 | H | L | 3.0 |

# SCORING INSTRUCTIONS FOR DISCRIMINATION INDEX

The discrimination score may be determined as follows:

1. Subtract the prospective teacher's ratings from the trained rater's ratings.

2. Disregarding signs, add the deviation scores.

3. Divide the total deviation score by the number of ratings to obtain the average deviation.

Here is an illustration:

| Trained Rater's Ratings | | Teacher's Ratings | | Deviation |
|---|---|---|---|---|
| 1.0 | - | 2.0 | = | 1 |
| 4.0 | - | 3.0 | = | 1 |
| 3.0 | - | 2.0 | = | 1 |
| 2.0 | - | 4.0 | = | 2 |
| 5.0 | - | 3.0 | = | 2 |

Total          7 $\div$ 5 = 1.40

Discrimination Score          = 1.40

The average deviation yields the discrimination score. It tells us how much the prospective teacher deviates from trained raters in his ratings. Discrimination scores of one-half (1/2) level or less deviation are good scores. It means that the prospective teacher's ratings do not deviate much from the trained rater's ratings. What one calls helpful, the other calls helpful. What one calls harmful, the other calls harmful. Discrimination scores over one (1) level deviation are poor scores. Teachers and raters do not see the same things happening.

The items where the prospective teacher deviates most from the raters are of greatest interest. Prospective teachers will tend to deviate most on L-H items where the teachers' responses are high on initiative (action-orientation) but low on responsiveness (understanding). Direction without understanding is of limited value.

BIBLIOGRAPHY

Aspy, D. N.
Toward a Technology for Humanizing
Education Champaign, Illinois:
Research Press, 1972.
Useful for understanding the
research base for the facili-
tative interpersonal dimensions of the Carkhuff Model in
education. Contains introduc-
tions to Flanders Interaction
Analysis and Bloom's cognitive
processes as well as empathy,
congruence and regard. Concludes that teachers with high
levels of interpersonal skills
have students who achieve more.

Aspy, D. N. and Roebuck, F.N.
Kids Don't Learn from People They
Don't Like Amherst, Massachusetts:
Human Resource Development Press,
1977.
Useful for understanding the
research base for the Carkhuff
Model in teaching. Studies the
differential effects of training in Flanders, Bloom and
Carkhuff skills. Hundreds of
teachers were trained. The
effects on thousands of learners were studied. Significant
gains were achieved on the following indices: student absen-
teeism and tardiness; student
discipline and school crises;
student learning skills and
cognitive growth. Concludes that
the Carkhuff model is the preferred teacher training model.

Berenson, B. G.
Belly-to-Belly and Back-to-Back
The Militant Humanism of Robert R.
Carkhuff Amherst, Massachusetts:
Human Resource Development Press,
1975.
Useful for an understanding of
the human assumptions under-
lying the human and educational
resource development models of
Carkhuff. Presents a collection
of prose and poetry by Carkhuff.
Concludes by challenging us to
die growing.

Berenson, B. G. and Carkhuff, R. R.
The Sources of Gain in Counseling and
Psychotherapy New York: Holt,
Rinehard and Winston, 1967.
Useful for an in-depth view of
the different orientations to
helping. Integrates the research of diverse approaches to
helping. Concludes with a model
of core conditions around which
the different preferred modes of
treatment make their own unique
contributions to helpee benefits.

Berenson, B. G. and Mitchell, K. M.
Confrontation: For Better of Worse
Amherst, Massachusetts: Human
Resource Development Press, 1974
Useful for an in-depth view of
confrontation and immediacy as
well as the core interpersonal
dimensions. Presents extensive
experimental manipulation of
core interpersonal skills and
confrontation and immediacy.

Concludes that while confrontation is never necessary and never sufficient, in the hands of an effective helper it may be efficient for moving the helpee toward constructive gain or change.

Berenson, D. H., Berenson, S. R. and Carkhuff, R. R.
The Skills of Teaching - Content Development Skills
Amherst, Massachusetts: Human Resource Development Press, in press, 1978.
Useful for learning skills needed for developing teaching content. Develops skills-based content in terms of do and think steps and supportive knowledge in terms of facts, concepts and principles. Concludes that content must be developed programmatically in order to ensure teaching delivery.

Berenson, S. R.; Carkhuff, R. R.; Berenson, D. H. and Pierce, R. M.
The Do's and Don'ts of Teaching
Amherst, Massachusetts: Human Resource Development Press, 1977.
Use for pre-service and in-service teachers. Lays out the interpersonal skills of teaching and their effect in the most basic form. Concludes that effective teachers apply skills that facilitate their learners' involvement in learning.

Carkhuff, R. R.
Helping and Human Relations. Vol. 1. Selection and Training Vol. 2. Practice and Research
New York: Holt, Rinehard and Winston, 1969.
Useful for understanding the research base for interpersonal skills in counseling and education. Operationalizes the helping process in great detail. Presents extensive research evidence for systematic selection, training and treatment procedures. Concludes that teaching is the preferred mode of treatment for helping.

Carkhuff, R. R.
The Development of Human Resources: Education, Psychology and Social Change New York: Holt, Rinehart and Winston, 1971.
Useful for understanding applications of human resource development (HRD) models. Describes and presents research evidence for numerous applications in helping skills training in human, educational and community resource development. Concludes that systematic planning for human delivery systems can be effectively translated into human benefits.

Carkhuff, R. R.
The Art of Helping III
Amherst, Massachusetts: Human

Resources Development Press, 3rd Edition, 1977.

Useful for learning helping skills. Includes attending, responding personalizing and initiating modules. Concludes that helping is a way of life.

Carkhuff, R. R. and Berenson, B. G.
Beyond Counseling and Therapy
New York: Holt, Rinehard and Winston, 2nd Edition, 1977

Useful for understanding of the core interpersonal conditions and their implications and applications. Adds many core dimensions and factors them out as responsive and initiative dimensions. Includes an analysis of the client-centered, existential, psychoanalytic, trait-and-factor and behavioristic orientations to helping. Concludes that only the trait-and-factor and behavioristic positions make unique contributions to human benefits over and above the core conditions.

Carkhuff, R. R. and Berenson, B. G.
Teaching As Treatment
Amherst, Massachusetts: Human Resource Development Press, 1976.

Useful for understanding the development of a human technology. Operationalizes the helping process as teaching. Offers research evidence for living, learning and working skills development and physical, emotional and intellectual outcomes. Concludes that learning-to-learn is the fundamental model for living, learning and working.

Carkhuff, R. R.; Berenson, D. H. and Berenson, S. R.
The Skills of Teaching - Lesson Planning Skills
Amherst, Massachusetts: Human Resource Development Press, in press, 1978.

Useful for learning skills needed to prepare for delivering content. Organizes lessons by reviewing, overviewing, presenting, exercising and summarizing. Breaks the organization down into a tell-show-do format. Concludes that content must be delivered in programmatic ways in order to maximize learning.

Carkhuff, R. R.; Devine, J.; Berenson, B. G.; Griffin, A. H.; Angelone, R.; Keeling, T.; Patch, W. and Steinberg, H.
Cry Twice
Amherst, Massachusetts: Human Resource Development Press, 1973.

Useful for understanding the ingredients of institutional change. Details the people, programs and organizational variables needed to transform

v

an institution from a custodial to a treatment orientation.  Concludes that institutional change begins with
people change.

Carkhuff, R. R. and Pierce, R. M.
    Teacher As Person
    Washington, D. C.:  National Educa-
    tion Association, 1976.
        Useful for teachers interested
        in ameliorating the effects
        of sexism and racism.  Includes
        modules and applications of
        interpersonal skills in the
        school.  Concludes that be-
        haviors teachers practice in-
        fluence learning which stu-
        dents achieve.

Rogers, C. R.; Gendlin, E. T.; Kiesler,
D., Truax, C. B.
    The Therapeutic Relationship and
    Its Impact
    Madison, Wisconsin:  University of
    Wisconsin Press, 1967.
        Useful for understanding the
        transitional phases in develop-
        ing HRD models.  Presents ex-
        tensive evidence on train-
        ing lay and professional
        helpers as well as different
        orientations to helping.  Con-
        cludes that the core inter-
        personal dimensions of
        empathy, respect and genui-
        neness are critical to effec-
        tive helping.

Truax, C. B. and Carkhuff, R. R.
    Toward Effective Counseling and
    Therapy
    Chicago, Illinois:  Aldine, 1967
        Useful for understanding the
        historical roots of the HRD
        models.  Presents extensive
        evidence on client-centered
        counseling for schizophrenic
        patients.  Concludes that
        core interpersonal dimensions
        of empathy, regard and con-
        gruence are critical to effec-
        tive helping.

other
publications
from Human
Resource
Development
Press

## LIVING SKILLS

### THE ART OF HELPING III

By Robert Carkhuff, Richard Pierce and John Cannon. Completely revised for 1977! This best-selling interpersonal skills text is now even better. There's a new helping model, more skill steps, built-in pre-post tests, more realistic illustrations, new practice exercises and examples of actual helping interviews. It's clean format and straightforward style make for easy reading. And it still breaks this complex subject into easy-to-learn steps. Designed for anyone interested in relating more helpfully to people. 196 pp., annotated bibliography, 190 illus., 8½ x 5½", spiral bound, $5.95.

### HELPING III – TRAINER'S GUIDE

By Robert Carkhuff, Richard Pierce, et al. Also revised for 1977! Contains training techniques for people who teach helpers. Based on over 15 years of experience teaching interpersonal skills. Includes tips on planning a training program, exercises for skill development, outside assignments for skill application and evaluation tools. Has *The Art of Helping III* reprinted inside for easy reference. A real time-saver! 170 pp., annotated bibliography, 8½ x 11", paper, $9.95.

### THE ART OF PROBLEM SOLVING

By Robert Carkhuff. A manual for developing decision-making skills. Includes sections on defining problems, defining goals, developing values, plus selecting and implementing courses of action. Uses a case study approach and clear step-by-step exercises to teach this skill. Designed for anyone who needs a simple, systematic technique for approaching complex decisions. 143 pp., 140 illus., 8½ x 5½", spiral bound, $5.95.

### HOW TO HELP YOURSELF

By Robert Carkhuff. A manual for building program development and implementation skills. For people who need to learn how to systematically plan and follow programs. Chapters on self-diagnosis, defining goals, developing steps to reach goals and implementing action plans. Features scales to assess physical, emotional and intellectual human functioning, plus case study examples. 172 pp., 160 illus. 8½ x 5½", spiral bound, $5.95.

## RESEARCH AND PERSPECTIVE

### TEACHING AS TREATMENT

By Robert Carkhuff and Bernard Berenson. A textbook presentation of the research evidence and rationale for operationalizing "teaching as the preferred mode of helping." Written for teaching and helping personnel who want to stay on the cutting edge of their field. Offers research evidence for living, learning and working skills development with resulting physical, emotional and intellectual outcomes. Concludes with a comprehensive design for educational delivery systems. 286 pp., references, 50 illus. and 36 tables, 6 x 9", paper, $9.95.

### BELLY-TO-BELLY, BACK-TO-BACK:

By Bernard Berenson. A collection of essays, stories and poetry by Robert Carkhuff with commentaries by Dr. Berenson. These writings (some previously unpublished) provide an intimate look inside "Carkhuff the person." Written for anyone interested in the ethic, values and assumptions of Carkhuff and the emerging Human Technology movement. 102 pp., 6 x 9", paper, $6.95.

### CONFRONTATION: FOR BETTER OR WORSE!

By Bernard Berenson and Kevin Mitchell. This text provides you with a summary of a decade of research on confrontation, an in-depth view of its uses and abuses, and the perspective necessary to use the skill constructively. This is *the* definitive work on this subject to date! 106 pp., references, 15 tables, 6 x 9", paper, $6.95.

### CRY TWICE!

The Story of Operation Changeover

By Robert Carkhuff, et al. This is an in-depth case study of the process and ingredients of successful institutional change. It details the people, program and organizational variables that needed to be changed to transform an institution from a custodial to a treatment orientation. All this and a good story too! 128 pp., 15 illus., 6 x 9", paper, $6.95.

Mix and match titles for a discount on **prepaid** orders only: 2-4 books 10%; 5 or more 15%.

## TEACHING SKILLS

### THE SKILLS OF TEACHING: INTERPERSONAL SKILLS

By Robert Carkhuff, David Berenson and Richard Pierce. Hailed as ". . . a landmark in educational technology", this text is the most advanced book available to teach both education students and teachers the basic interpersonal skills they need to teach effectively. Covered are attending skills, responding skills, personalizing skills and initiating skills. This book features exercises to help the reader learn and apply the skills, pre-post tests for immediate feedback, a straightforward style and open format for easy reading; plus 60 photographs to illustrate the skills in actual use. Teachers love it! 206 pp., annotated bibliography, 60 illus., paper, $6.95.

### DO'S AND DON'TS OF TEACHING

By Sally Berenson, Robert Carkhuff, David Berenson and Richard Pierce. This handbook of simplified interpersonal skills was written for student teachers and new teachers in the field who are looking for concrete guidelines for what to *do* and *not do* in the classroom. This book features sketches to illustrate the good and bad techniques, a clear, easy-to-read style and skills that are immediately applicable to any classroom or learning situation. 120 pp., 5½ x 8½", paper, $3.95.

## FITNESS SKILLS

### GET FIT FOR LIVING

By Tom Collingwood and Robert Carkhuff. A text designed to teach you how to develop individualized physical fitness programs based upon your present physical condition and your unique goals. Includes skills for self-assessment, setting goals, plus developing and implementing fitness programs to increase your endurance, strength and flexibility. Written for helpers, parents, teachers and everyone who needs a high level of physical energy. 100pp.,6x9", paper,$3.95

### GET FIT TRAINER'S GUIDE

By Tom Collingwood and Robert Carkhuff. This is a training manual that details methods for teaching fitness skills. To help save you time in preparation it includes: complete lesson plans, how to develop personalized fitness programs and what you need to know about exercise and the body. 272 pp., bibliography, 6x9", $9.95.

## WORKING SKILLS

### GETAJOB!

By Robert Carkhuff, Richard Pierce, Ted Friel and David Willis. This is a handbook for anyone who wants to land a job. *GETAJOB!* teaches you the skills you need to identify assets from both your school and work experiences, find job openings before they're advertised, write powerful resumes and personal cover letters and control the job interview. It features step-by-step instructions, with examples, case studies and room to write in the book for permanent reference. After reading *GETAJOB!*, you'll never need help in finding a job again! 178 pp., 7 x 10", paper, $6.95.

### CAREER STUDENT'S GUIDE

By Robert Carkhuff and Ted Friel. This workbook teaches you exactly how to develop your career. Chapters on Career Expanding, Narrowing and Planning Skills give you the tools. Hundreds of exercises, examples of each step, plus thousands of job titles insure that you won't need outside help to plan your path through life. 229 pp., 8½ x 11", paper, $6.95.

### CAREER HELPER'S GUIDE

By Ted Friel and Robert Carkhuff. This guide is a collection of techniques that helpers, counselors and teachers can use to teach career skills to students. Included are methods you can use to involve students in exploring, understanding and acting upon their careers. For your convenience, the *Student's Guide* has been reprinted inside this version. The entire book will save you time when teaching students how to plan their lives. 323 pp., 8½ x 11", paper, $9.95.

### JUNIOR HIGH CAREER COMIC

By Ted Friel and Robert Carkhuff. Scaled-down version of the above career books designed especially for Jr. High students. Helps make school work more relevant for students. 63 pp., illus. 8½ x 11", $3.95.

## APPLICATIONS

### THE ART OF HEALTH CARE

By William Anthony and Robert Carkhuff. Teaches the kind of interpersonal skills health care professionals need to do their job well. This text-workbook uses the vocabulary and discusses the unique problems that face nurses, physical and occupational therapists and doctors each day. Also overviews decision-making and planning skills to provide the ideal training manual for both in-service and pre-service training. 104 pp., 6 x 9", paper, $4.95.

### HELPING BEGINS AT HOME

By Robert Carkhuff and Richard Pierce. This handbook of basic parenting skills is designed to be used with parents who want to learn how to make their families more effective. The physical, emotional and intellectual skills covered will lead to increased energy levels, improved interpersonal relationships and better planned lives. It features an enjoyable story of a typical family that needs and uses these easily learned and effective skills. 121 pp., 6 x 9", paper, $3.95.

### TEACHER AS PERSON

By Robert Carkhuff and Richard Pierce. This manual is designed to teach interpersonal skills to teachers who wish to avoid the ill effects of racism and sexism in their classrooms. Discusses the multicultural implications of these skills and shows how their use prevents racism and sexism. 64 pp., 9 x 10", paper, $3.50.

### ELEMENTARY CAREER COMIC

By Robert Carkhuff and Ted Friel. Scaled-down version of the above career books designed especially for elementary school students, grades 4-6. 48 pp., illus., 8½ x 11", $3.45.

## THE HRD AUDIOTAPE SERIES

By Robert Carkhuff. Each of the following tape packages is a set of recorded tests to be used to measure an individual's ability to communicate and discriminate effective interpersonal skills. These packages can be used by trainers to evaluate skill gains due to training; by researchers to measure levels of interpersonal skills in different populations; and by graduate students as a valid measure for masters or doctoral level applied research. Each of the four packages contains 16 helpee stimulus problems with 5 helper responses to each problem. The items have been grouped for ease of use when pre-post testing. The problems have been choosen from a range of problems typical to each setting. Also included is a booklet with a complete transcript of the tape, directions for its use and a summary of the research behind the tapes and the Carkhuff Scales. These tapes will save time by providing you with a readily available measure of interpersonal skills functioning. Each tape has 2 sides, ½ hour per side and costs $25.00.

### COUNSELOR-COUNSELEE PACKAGE

is designed to be used in settings concerned with counseling and guidance activities like high schools, colleges, community mental health centers and paraprofessional training programs.

### TEACHER-STUDENT PACKAGE

is designed to be used with individuals involved with students like: teachers, teacher's aides, school nurses, coaches, administrators, principals and anyone else whose work involves student contact.

### CORRECTIONAL HELPER-INMATE PACKAGE

is designed to be used with correctional officers, counselors, administrators and others whose work centers on inmates in either juvenile or adult correctional settings.

### HUMAN RELATIONS PACKAGE

is designed to be used in any of the above settings where either racism or sexism issues are of particular concern.

## ORDERING INFORMATION

1. **TO ORDER** Send list of titles and payment (check or money order) to:
   HRD Press
   Box 863 Dept. M 41
   Amherst, MA 01002

2. **TERMS:** Payment with order unless accompanied by official institutional purchase order. We pay fourth class postage on all prepaid orders.

3. **DISCOUNTS** for prepaid orders of more than one book; mix and match titles as you wish!

   | | |
   |---|---|
   | 1 book | 0% |
   | 2-4 books | 10% |
   | 5 or more | 15% |

4. **FOR EXTRA FAST DELIVERY** enclose 35¢ per book for UPS or 75¢ per book for 1ST CLASS MAIL. When using a purchase order full postage will be charged.

5. **WHEN ORDERING VIDEOTAPES** please specify make and model number of your machine and tape size (½" EIAJ, ¾" UMATIC CASSETTE, 1" AMPEX). Please write for our Videotape Brochure for information on previewing these tapes.

6. **BOOKSTORES ONLY:** 20% discount on all titles, shipped prepaid, FOB Lawrence, MA. Returns must be authorized in advance. See NACS Trade-Text Manual for complete policy. Invoices not paid within 30 days of end of month billed will lose discount.

7. **DESK COPIES** or Teacher's Guides (when available) are sent only to adopting professors upon receipt of a photocopy of their class order for 20 or more copies of a title.

8. **COMPLIMENTARY EXAMINATION COPIES** for the purpose of review for possible adoption will be sent if you are currently teaching, or within the next year, plan to teach a course for which one of our texts is appropriate. Requests for complimentary examination copies must be on letterhead and include course title and number, current text, adoption decision date and approximate enrollment.

9. *All prices subject to change without notice.*

## THE HRD VIDEOTAPE SERIES

By Robert Carkhuff. Includes three levels of training videotapes produced to be used with any population above the 10th grade level. Each tape is in black and white and features Dr. Carkhuff as a model for effective helping and training. Each module has built-in pre-post tests and a lecture-demonstration-practice delivery format. As a series, they will add to any trainer's understanding of training techniques and principles, plus offer a non-threatening means for introducing the Carkhuff Model in your skills training. Finally, they allow you to stop the action to discuss key points and can save you time by allowing your trainees to independently review and preview specific skills.

### THE LIFE SKILLS MODEL VIDEOTAPES

include three basic training modules to introduce the Carkhuff Model:

### Helping Model Module

introduces the basic interpersonal skills of the Carkhuff model including Attending, Responding, Personalizing and Initiating. 1 hour, $250.00.

### Problem Solving Model Module

reviews the Carkhuff Model and teaches the skills involved in decision-making. 1 hour, $250.00.

### Program Development Model Module

reviews the Carkhuff Model and then teaches the skills involved in program development. 1 hour, $250.00.

## THE ART OF HELPING TRAINING VIDEOTAPES

include four intermediate level training modules which treat the basic interpersonal skills in more depth:

### Attending Skills Module

teaches the specific skills of attending physically, observing and listening. ½ hour, $200.00.

### Responding Skills Module

teaches the skills of responding to content, responding to feelings and responding to feeling and content. ½ hour, $200.00.

### Personalizing Skills Module

teaches the skills involved in personalizing meaning, personalizing the problem and feeling, plus personalizing the goal. ½ hour, $200.00.

### Initiating Skills Module

teaches the skills trainees need to operationalize helpee goals and develop steps to achieve these goals. ½ hour, $200.00.

## THE ART OF HELPING DEMONSTRATION VIDEOTAPES

include three taped interviews with Dr. Carkhuff demonstrating the use of all of the above skills:

### The Case of Jerry

involves a young man who must make an important life decision. Dr. Carkhuff utilizes interpersonal, decision-making and program development skills in this interview. 1 hour, $250.00.

### The Case of Manny

involves another young man who is experiencing social and interpersonal difficulties. Dr. Carkhuff utilizes advanced responsive and immediacy skills in this tape. 1 hour, $250.00 (not available after 9/1/77).

### The Case of Jane

is an interview with a young mother who is having child-rearing problems. Dr. Carkhuff illustrates the use of basic responsive and initiative skills. 3/4 hour, $200.00 (not available after 9/1/77).

The above videotapes are available for purchase only. Each tape can be ordered in one of three tape sizes: ½" EIAJ, ¾" UMATIC Cassette, and 1" AMPEX. Write for our *Videotape Brochure* for more information on previewing, discount policy and other uses for these tapes.

# order form

**Helping Model Module** $250.00

|  |  |
|---|---|
| Problem Solving Model Module | 250.00 |
| Program Development Model Module | 250.00 |
| Life Skills Videotape Set (above 3) | 635.00 |

**Art of Helping Training Videotapes**

|  |  |
|---|---|
| Attending Skills | 200.00 |
| Responding Skills | 200.00 |
| Personalizing Skills | 200.00 |
| Initiating Skills | 200.00 |
| Art of Helping Training Videotape Set (above 4) | 675.00 |

**Art of Helping Demonstration Videotapes**

|  |  |
|---|---|
| The Case of Jerry | 250.00 |
| The Case of Jane | 200.00 |
| The Case of Manny | 250.00 |
| Art of Helping Demonstration Videotape Set (above 3) | 595.00 |

**Videotape Sets**

|  |  |
|---|---|
| Any two of the above sets (25% discount) | 1125.00 |
| All three of above sets (35% discount) | 1460.00 |

**HRD Audiotape Series**

|  |  |
|---|---|
| Teacher-Student Tape Package | 25.00 |
| Counselor-Counselee Tape Package | 25.00 |
| Correctional Helper-Inmate Tape Package | 25.00 |
| Human Relations: Sexism/Racism Tape Package | 25.00 |
| HRD Audiotape Set (above 4) | 75.00 |

## BOOKS

**Research and Perspective**

|  |  |
|---|---|
| Kids Don't Learn from People They Don't Like | 11.95 |
| Teaching As Treatment | 9.95 |
| Belly-to-Belly, Back-to-Back | 6.95 |
| Confrontation: For Better or Worse | 6.95 |
| Cry Twice | 6.95 |

**Living Skills**

|  |  |
|---|---|
| The Art of Helping III | 5.95 |
| The Art of Problem Solving | 5.95 |
| The Art of Program Development | 5.95 |
| The Art of Helping III - Trainer's Guide | 9.95 |

**Teaching Skills**

|  |  |
|---|---|
| The Do's and Don'ts of Teaching | 3.95 |
| The Skills of Teaching: Interpersonal Skills | 6.95 |
| The Skills of Teaching: Interpersonal Skills Teacher's Guide | 9.95 |

**Working Skills**

|  |  |
|---|---|
| GETAJOB | 6.95 |
| The Art of Developing a Career | 6.95 |
| The Art of Developing a Career - Helper's Guide | 9.95 |
| Junior High Career Comic | 3.95 |
| Elementary School Career Comic | 3.45 |

**Fitness Skills**

|  |  |
|---|---|
| Get Fit for Living | 4.95 |
| Get Fit for Living - Trainer's Guide | 6.95 |

**Applications**

|  |  |
|---|---|
| The Art of Health Care | 4.95 |
| IPC: Skills for Correctional Management | 5.95 |
| IPC: Trainer's Guide | 9.95 |
| Helping Begins at Home | 3.95 |
| Teacher As Person | 3.50 |

SUBTOTAL

Minus Discount -

Mass. Residents add 5% Sales Tax +

Postage for Extra Fast delivery +

Amount enclosed $ ____ check or money order

Payment or purchase order must accompany this order.

MAKE CHECK PAYABLE TO "HRD PRESS" AND SEND IT WITH THIS ORDER FORM TO: **HRD Press**, Box 863, Dept. M41, Amherst, MA 01002

Name _____

Address _____

City _____ State _____ Zip _____

HRD Press, Box 863, Dept. M41
Amherst, MA 01002 (413) 253-3488

371.102

C277,2

Teachers' Guide

118 792

| DATE DUE | | | |
|---|---|---|---|
| | | | |
| | | | |
| | | | |
| | | | |
| | | | |
| | | | |
| | | | |
| | | | |
| | | | |
| | | | |
| | | | |
| | | | |
| | | | |
| | | | |
| | | | |
| | | | |
| | | | |
| | | | |
| | | | |
| GAYLORD | | | PRINTED IN U.S.A. |